SOCIAL EUROPE

The labour market for information technology professionals in Europe

DOCUMENTS OFFICIELS

APR 2 2 1992

GOVERNMENT PUBLICATIONS

SUPPLEMENT 1/90

COMMISSION OF THE EUROPEAN COMMUNITIES

DIRECTORATE-GENERAL FOR EMPLOYMENT, INDUSTRIAL RELATIONS AND SOCIAL AFFAIRS

This publication is also available in the following languages:

DE ISBN 92-826-1228-7
FR ISBN 92-826-1230-9

The information contained in this publication does not necessarily reflect either the position or views of the Commission of the European Communities.

Luxembourg, Office for Official Publications of the European Communities, 1990

© ECSC—EEC—EAEC, Brussels • Luxembourg, 1990
Reproduction is authorized, except for commercial purposes, provided the source is acknowledged.

Catalogue number: CE-NC-90-001-EN-C

ISBN 92-826-1229-5

Printed in Belgium

CONTENTS

	Page
Editorial	1
The job market for computer professionals in Europe	3
Belgium	21
Denmark	41
Federal Republic of Germany	59
Greece	73
Spain	77
France	87
Ireland	99
Italy	105
Luxembourg	115
The Netherlands	121
Portugal	135
United Kingdom	143
Selected Bibliography	157

EDITORIAL

There are many good reasons for taking an interest in the job market for computer professionals. Of all the various professions linked to new information technology, computing provides a classic example of jobs created as a result of technological developments. What's more, computer-related professions are witnessing a huge upsurge in popularity in all the various education systems; they also provide unmistakable evidence of the growing role played by data processing within organizations. Finally, it is a well-known fact that Europe is currently suffering from a relative shortage of computer specialists, thus creating a tense, volatile situation in the market for these particular skills.

The prospect of European integration would seem, once again, to highlight the need for a comparative approach to the recent development of computer-related professions within the EC.

This overview has been compiled on the basis of twelve national reports, prepared by correspondents employed by the EPOS network on "New technologies and social change in Europe" (1). It is followed by a summary of each of these twelve national reports.

---

(1) The network of EPOS correspondents consists of G. Valenduc (B), N. Bjorn-Andersen (DK), J. Palacio Moreno (E), N. Azoulay (F), M. Nikolanikos (GR), M.E. J. O'Kelly (IRL), P. Piacentini (I), J. Kintzele (L), D. van der Werf (NL), L. Tadeu Almeida (P) and T. Brady (UK). The summary was compiled by G. Valenduc, who also decided on the final format of the national reports (in association with M. Poskin). The co-ordinators representing the EC Commission are L.E. Andreasen and H. De Jong.

THE JOB MARKET FOR COMPUTER PROFESSIONALS
IN EUROPE

1. WHO ARE THE "COMPUTER PROFESSIONALS"?

The problem of defining professions

There is no single, internationally recognized definition or criterion which would allow us to pinpoint the various types of computer professionals working in Europe. Each country classifies these professions in one or more ways and, in many cases, these classifications are not even used for statistical purposes.

In spite of the lack of a single, uniform approach, a certain convergence can be said to exist in the description of six main "families" of professions:

a) **"systems design"**: professions linked to the overall management of systems and networks, software or hardware engineering, network engineering, the design of data bases;

b) **"projects and applications"**: professions involving the design, development, management, analysis and planning of computer projects;

c) **"user support"**: activities associated with the monitoring of applications, user training and the role of "data processing correspondent";

d) **"operation"**: the management, organization, running and maintenance of data processing centres;

e) **"distribution"**: the marketing and selling of hardware and software, technical assistance for clients and after-sales service;

f) **"research"**: scientific jobs involving R&D, in the field of information technology.

In most Member States, categories (e) and, in particular, (f) are not included in the computer specialist classifications: being respectively regarded as commercial and scientific professions. Category (c) covers very recent functions which are not always regarded as professions in their own right and which are therefore rarely listed as such. Category (d) is the only one to enjoy a uniform definition throughout the Community. Traditionally, it includes computer centre management functions, even though such functions are increasingly associated with "systems management" and, hence, with category (a) activities.

The distinction between categories (a) and (b) is not always easy to make - for two reasons. Firstly, abuse of the term "system" causes considerable semantic confusion : for example, a systems engineer will often be a designer of networks or operating systems, while a systems analyst is more likely to design projects and applications for users. Furthermore, the degree to which labour is divided - and hence the degree of specialization within the professions - between systems design on the one hand and the design and development of applications on the other varies greatly depending on the type and size of the firms concerned, and the extent of national and sectoral computerization.

Different classification systems

Some national classifications are much more detailed than the summary breakdown given above. An examination of all the various classifications employed in the twelve national reports, reveals three methods of categorizing computer professions, which may be described as extensive, comprehensive and rudimentary.

In countries like the Federal Republic of Germany, Belgium, Denmark or the Netherlands recent, very detailed classifications are available incorporating 25 to 30 headings, which are sometimes combined in a smaller number of "professional categories". These provide an <u>extensive definition</u> of the various professions prepared by the public or semi-public institutions that are responsible for monitoring the job market. The fact that the definitions exist does not mean that they are used to record jobs; the classification devised by the Belgian National Employment Office is not used in any statistics.

In Great Britain, the Institute for Manpower Studies (IMS) has devised a <u>comprehensive definition</u> of the computer professions, by conflating definitions based on degrees awarded and definitions linked to functions performed within firms. This dual-input grid gives rise to some ten dominant professions, out of sixty or so possible combinations. The classification devised in France by the Research Centre for Employment and Qualifications (CEREQ) derives from a similar approach. When professions are defined on this comprehensive basis, there are fewer categories and the quantitative data are less fragmented; data quality is, however, often better in the case of a classification which is less detailed but more operationally-orientated.

One should not, therefore, overlook the merits of those rudimentary classification systems covering no more than three to five professional categories in use in Italy, Ireland and Portugal. Quite apart from the fact that such classifications may be more suitable to the state of computer development in some of the countries concerned, they offer a greater degree of long-term stability and facilitate comparison with other surveys.

The variety of classifications is a significant factor: it indicates the extent to which the public monitoring institutions or employment watchdog bodies are capable of defining and quantifying jobs in the information technology sector.

Diverse statistical sources

None of the national reports quotes a set of coherent statistical sources which would enable an overall view of the job market for computer professionals to be obtained without difficulty.

In many European countries, official statistics are not tailored to take account of such new and rapidly changing professions as IT occupations. As a result, the degree of consistency between statistics relating to employment and those relating to the education system is rarely satisfactory. Uniform data on "stocks" (existing jobs) and "flux"
(vacancies and job applications) are even harder to find.

As regards private studies, a large number of surveys have been conducted by computer consultants and manufacturers themselves, usually as a backu-up to their own intervention on the job market. Without wishing to detract from these surveys, it should be borne in mind that they are often restricted to certain areas of activity or professional categories, frequently not readily available to researchers and are rarely of any use for the compilation of chronological series. In those countries where official statistics and surveys would appear to be most inadequate (Belgium, Greece, Ireland), the data contained in certain private studies are indispensable for an accurate description of the job market for computer specialists.

Over the past three years, major efforts have been made in some countries to improve existing knowledge of the computer professions and to forecast trends in the job market for the specialists concerned. Specific tasks have been assigned to public or semi-public research centres, which have proceeded to publish key reports: in 1986, the CHIP report(2) in the Netherlands, the CENSIS study(3) in Italy and the IMS study(4) in Great Britain, in 1987 the CEREQ report(5) in France and the FUNDESCO report(6) in Spain. The results of the CHIPS project (Computer History: Interdependencies, Power Strategies and Structures) in Denmark will also soon be available.

All these reports testify to the keen interest taken by several Member States in the various social, economic and educational issues associated with the development of the IT professions.

The disparate nature of the quantitative data poses a major difficulty when it comes to drawing comparisons at European level. For this reason, this document will focus on the principal job market trends and the qualitative aspects of the development of the various professions.

---

(2) CHIP Commissie voor Hoger Onderwijs Informatica Plan: Eindrapport, Den Haag, 1986.

(3) CENSIS (Centro Studi Investimenti Sociali), Informatica Italia 1986: mercato del lavoro, F. Angeli, Milano, 1987

(4) Connor H. and Pearon R. Information Technology Manpower into the 1990's Institute for Manpower Studies (IMS) April 1986.

(5) CEREQ Jobs in Computing (2 vol.). Centre of Research Centre for Employment and Qualifications. French Documentation, Paris 1987.

(6) FUNDESCO (Fundacion para el desarrollo social de las communicaciones). Formacion de técnicos e investigadores en technologias de la informacion: analisis de la oferta y la demanda de estos professionales en Espana Madrid, 1986.

2. THE JOB MARKET FOR COMPUTER PROFESSIONALS

An upsurge in the popularity of computer studies

Since the early Eighties, the number of degrees awarded in computer studies has begun to grow at a faster pace (15 to 20% per year) both in universities and other higher education establishments. For example, the number of graduates in computer studies, virtually doubled in Germany, Belgium, France and Spain between 1982 and 1986.

The range of studies in the field of information technology greatly expanded over this period, particularly in the case of applied and management computing. In countries like France, the United Kingdom, Ireland, Germany or the Netherlands, the authorities introduced medium-term plans aimed specifically at increasing resources for training computer specialists.

Although the general trend is undoubtedly towards an increase in the number of graduates, several particular points should be noted. Thus, the increase is currently much more noticeable in the case of university studies than in that of short term higher education courses; in Belgium and Italy, for example, the number of students enrolled in the latter is already beginning to level off. On the other hand, conversion and post-graduate courses in computing which enable graduates from other disciplines to acquire a second qualification in a short time, are currently undergoing rapid expansion in several countries.

Course content varies from country to country: whereas the training of specialists in new information technologies is still heavily geared towards electronics, mathematics or engineering in Italy, Spain, Portugal or Ireland, it tends to be more closely associated with management science in Denmark and France.

As we shall see, young computer graduates experience few problems finding employment. Even in the case of the least sought-after qualifications (programming and operating) overall demand still outstrips the number of students leaving full-time education.

Finally, the reason for this recent increase in the number of degrees in computing lies in the fact that, during the Sixties and Seventies, firms were very often computerized by people who were not themselves qualified computer specialists but who had received on-the-job training from manufacturers or service companies. Similarly, programming and operating staff often acquired their qualifications through vocational training. This explains why, in the case of existing occupations, computer science graduates continue to constitute a minority.

Jobs which remain concentrated in a few branches

In order to have a true understanding of the forces of supply and demand on the job market for computer professionals, it is important to gain some idea of the "stock" of existing jobs.

Firstly, it appears that existing jobs are concentrated in a few sectors: the computer industry itself, business services (including computer-related servicing and advice) and certain large user sectors such as banking and insurance, the Civil Service and retailing. Insofar as quantitative data can be compared from one country to another(7), the proportions are approximately as follows: 10 to 15% of computer-specialist jobs are in the electronics and data-processing industry, 10 to 15% are in service and consultancy companies and 70% to 75% are accounted for by user firms (with a ratio of approximately 1:2 between the manufacturing and services sectors).
France is something of an exception, since 25% of its computer specialists work for service and consultancy companies and this figure corresponds to the size of this particular branch in relation to the French economy as a whole.

Among the various "families" of professions, computer operators account for approximately one third of existing jobs. Analysis/programming and programming ("applications" subgroup) account for between 28 and 35%, while management and systems and networks design ("system" subgroup) account for between 30 and 38%. In the most recent studies, management functions, which constitute from 7 to 12% of the jobs(8), are often included in the latter subgroup.

---

(7) Data on the breakdown of jobs by sector are given in the Belgian, UK, Danish, French, Italian and Portuguese reports, but the studies mentioned deal with different years and sectors are classified in different ways.

(8) Data on the functional breakdown of jobs are given in the Belgian, UK, Danish, French and Portuguese reports while the Spanish and Italian reports deal with only a few branches; once again, the periods referred to are not the same. Reservations regarding the reliability of correlations between "families" of professions have already been mentioned.

Major discrepancies between supply and demand

In Germany, computer science graduates find themselves in a situation in which there are five available posts for every applicant; for students with lower qualifications, the ratio is reversed. In Spain, the FUNDESCO study shows that, over the period 1985-88, supply satisfied only 40% of the estimated demand. In France, although a government support plan for the electronics industry doubled the annual number of graduates between 1982 and 1986, and although this trend is continuing, it was not until 1988 that a quantitative balance between supply and demand was achieved. As far as quality is concerned, serious imbalances still persist.

These few examples underline the current dearth of skills on the job market; at the same time, they prompt consideration of the nature of the shortage. In all countries for which information is available, the unemployment rate for computer professionals remains stable at around 3%, whereas the demand for staff is increasing. This would seem to indicate structural unemployment, resulting from the permanent discrepancy between the qualifications which employers require and those which applicants actually hold.

The gap assumes different forms from one country to another. In France and Denmark, for example, the shortage of skills is most serious in the case of application analysts, whereas in Germany, Spain and the UK, system analysts tend to be the most highly sought-after specialists; in Belgium and the Netherlands, the shortage applies mainly to sales managers. Network specialists tend to be in short supply everywhere - although demand is limited. All of these situations would appear to have one thing in common: demand is clearly orientated towards the highest level of training (universities, polytechnics, business schools), whereas the job market for programmers is becoming far more stabilized. In countries where firms tend to be heavily computerized, the job market for computer operators is already saturated.

Moderately optimistic forecasts

None of the forecasts predict an end to the growth in demand for data processors. From now until 1990 or 1992, annual growth rates of between 10 and 15% are anticipated in all the countries in which such forecasts have been published, that is Spain, France, UK, the Netherlands. Compared with the early Eighties, growth is slower but continuing.

The accuracy of these forecasts is open to criticism. In Spain for instance, the projected growth rates for the last few years (1987-88) were too high in relation to actual job creation. In Holland, the level of demand predicted for 1990 in the CHIP report, and the changes in the education system introduced following its publication in 1985, could create a sudden "bottle-neck" on the job market.

Some graduates who have completed short courses in higher education (one or two years) are already confronted by a latent crisis. A typical example is provided by "data processing assistants" in Denmark, where the percentage of students who did not find a job immediately on completing their course increased from 43% to 69% between 1987 and 1988. Similar cases have been reported in France. nevertheless unemployment among computer specialists generally remains very low in all the Member States. Alongside the few cases of saturation, there are areas of the job market where recruiters are reduced to "poaching" and where the regulating mechanisms are linked to salaries and firms' personnel management policies.

Extreme salary-related pressure

Highly-qualified specialists, for whom the cyclical gap between supply and demand is wider than elsewhere, command the highest salaries: this group comprises systems and network designers (engineers and analysts) who have recently overtaken analyst/programmers as the highest earners. In these particular segments of the job market, salary levels and company benefits are the major regulatory factors and tend to determine mobility.

Insofar as they are known, salary scales for computer specialists appear to cover a very wide range; as the Belgian report points out, salaries are the subject of confidential studies conducted by specialist consultants who build up their own picture of the job market which they proceed to sell to firms(9).

The highest salaries are found in the computer services and consultancy sector of the industry and tend to be lowest in the public sector. As a general rule, data processors are better off in the service sector than in industry. The salaries paid to analyst/programmers and computer operators now appear to have levelled off.

---

(9) The German, Danish, French, Dutch and Portuguese reports refer to publications on the salaries paid to computer specialists in their respective countries.

Computer specialists are, on average, better paid than office workers and executives at the same level. Inequality between men and women tends to be less marked among computer specialists than other office workers, although the few statistics available in Denmark and Holland show that in every area of the computer industry, male employees earn more than their female counterparts.

Finally, it would appear that the regulatory role played by salaries is linked to the "life-cycle" of qualifications. Every time a new qualification emerges at the top end of the profession, a cyclical shortage ensues, thus causing salaries to soar. This is followed by a period of normalization, during which the new qualification gradually becomes more commonplace, and salaries begin to level off. Once the new qualification has finally been absorbed into existing professions, salary levels are largely determined by opportunities facilities for mobility and retraining.

None of this serves fully to explain the existing disparities between the different sectors. In order to gain a truer understanding of the phenomenon, a second regulating factor must be taken into account, namely the various recruitment strategies adopted by firms.

The internal and external job markets

The existence of a sort of "dual job market", both within and outside firms, was brought to light, in particular, by the studies conducted by CEREQ in France(10). On the external job market, firms can find the skills they require immediately if they are prepared to pay the price: salaries linked to the economic cycles, increased mobility, possible internal difficulties resulting from changing staff regulations. In an attempt to escape this excessive influence of market fluctuations, firms can organize their own internal job market by recruiting or selecting from their existing workforce staff who, although qualified, do not necessarily possess a computing background. They then invest heavily in in-house training, offering the prospect of a combined career, either within or outside the computer industry(11). This last-mentioned strategy is particularly favoured by large-scale user firms (banks and insurance companies, for example).

---

(10) Lochet J.F., Verdier E., Is there really a specific market for computer specialists? in "Training and employment" (CEREQ), n 17 (1987), French Documentation, Paris

(11) A qualitative description of these strategies can be found in the Belgian and Danish reports; the Italian and Dutch reports contain data which support this description.

The coexistence of these two recruitment strategies inevitably affects the link between training and employment for those working in the computer industry. The general trend is as follows: there is a clear correlation between the content of training courses and job requirements in the case of programmers and hardware and network specialists whereas no such correlation would seem to exist in the case of analysts and consultants.

In other words, selection criteria linked to the content of training courses are particularly important in the case of jobs in which the emphasis is on technical skills; on the other hand, criteria linked to the level and range of education received are more important in the case of jobs in which the ability to organize and relate to other people are paramount importance. This observation suggests a new explanatory factor for the development of the job market, namely the changing pattern of the professions themselves.

3. THE CHANGING PATTERN OF THE PROFESSIONS

Increasingly high qualification levels

Throughout the Community, the level of qualifications required of computer professionals is increasing as a result of several converging trends:
- the **"automation"** of the computer industry: with the advent of program generators, and the automation of formal specification procedures, the more up-to-date and repetitive programming and analysis functions call for fewer high-calibre programmers and even fewer analysts; training courses now focus increasingly on systems analysis and design, to the detriment of programming;
- the **"socialization"** of the computer industry: in addition to technical competence, computer specialists must now also offer a qualification in business organization, personnel management or business management; as the use of computers becomes increasingly widespread, new functions emerge, geared towards customer-support services;
- the **"refinement"** of information technology requirements with regard to education and experience are increasing in every type of profession; the growing complexity of networks and systems calls for a high degree of specialized knowledge coupled with considerable intellectual flexibility.

In some countries, these trends have given rise to conditions which have caused qualifications to become "polarized": this has meant that the qualifications of a minority of professionals have been up-graded, although it has meant the opposite for the majority. Programming and operating jobs are often cited as a classic example of the process of polarization. In Denmark, this theory was refuted in a comparative study[12] which shows that the division of labour between design and application is traditionally less marked in Denmark than in the UK and Japan, and that the organization systems adopted by Danish firms are more conducive to the integration of tasks such as project design, analysis and programming. Danish data processors prefer a more flexible approach to the division of labour and greater independence.

This Danish study makes the point that it is company organization systems and not just technology which determines the configuration of qualifications required. The Belgian, UK and French reports draw attention to the fact that job requirements for computer professionals depend heavily on the role of computerization in firms' reorganization strategies.

---

(12) Friedman A., <u>Strategies for computer people,</u> CHIPS Working Paper n 3, Copenhagen, Sept. 1987

Increased occupational mobility

The cyclical shortage on the job market and the "head-hunting" tactics practised by firms, have greatly enhanced the opportunities for occupational mobility.

The few statistics available show that mobility is not the preserve of highly qualified staff but that it also extends to programmers. The average turn-over rates are currently around 10 - 12% in France, the UK and Italy, though rates are far higher in the case of certain professional groups: 49% for analyst/programmers with between 3 and 5 years' experience in Italy, about 15% for programmers in France and UK and 13% for network engineers in France. French statistics show a decrease in mobility between 1981 and 1987. British statistics, meanwhile, show that mobility is more pronounced in London than elsewhere in the country and that the size of firms is also a significant factor, since mobility tends to be greater in small as opposal to large computer departments. The Danish report explains that mobility is particulary marked at the outset of employees' careers, when young specialists are anxious to compile a curriculum vitae which testifies to a wide range of experience.

A high degree of flexibility

The turnover rate among computer professionals does not, in itself, provide a satisfactory indication of occupational mobility. It is also necessary to take account of the wide range of service regulations and contracts of employment. Quite apart from the "conventional" staff who often benefit from an array of additional benefits, there are independent consultants, some of whom are linked to firms under exclusive employment contracts. Another alternative is the system of "temporary secondment", whereby manufacturers or service companies hire out computer specialists to user firms for a set period or for a specific job.
As far as working hours are concerned, overtime seems to be fairly well established, although quantitative information is rare. In Germany, three-quarters of computer professionals work more than 40 hours per week, while half work more than 45 hours. In Portugal, analysts work about 5 hours' overtime per week, although this would also appear to be the norm among other office workers.

Unstructured careers

The combined effects of the relative shortage of skills and increased mobility undoubtedly create good opportunities for "making a career" in the computer industry. Nevertheless, certain less favourable factors should also be mentioned.

Firstly, the job market for computer professionals is so volatile that there can be no stable career pattern. The Danish and French reports suggest that certain jobs (systems consultant, systems manager) were deliberately created to offer high-calibre specialists promotion prospects.

In addition, computer specialists may be led to pursue a career as executives, outside the computer industry. This is becoming increasingly common, as computer and user departments merge and firms set up an internal job market for their employees.

Finally, most of the national reports point out that career prospects are often insufficiently attractive in the public sector, particularly in the case of high-calibre specialists. On the other hand, the more "traditional" jobs (programming, operating) tend to be more secure in this area.

Problems with investment in training

Ever higher qualifications, routine mobility and the lack of a clearly defined career pattern mean that computer professionals constantly need to update their skills and that employers must invest heavily in continuing staff training.

A survey conducted in UK in 1984 shows that while 67% of firms had a computer training budget, only 51% pursued a training policy and no more than 39% maintained a training department. As in other countries, re-training is still often based on a teach-yourself approach, with the aid of textbooks or training packages; the Dutch report points out that the latter method, in particular, is under-utilized. Some employers and even some countries continue to begrudge spending money on training, refusing to regard it as a non-material investment.

In Germany, an opinion poll carried out by the professional association of computer specialists reveals considerable demand for re-training but widespread dissatisfaction (66%) with the available opportunities. The chief cause of this dissatisfaction is the lack of time available for training, owing to heavy workloads; the second reason is the reluctance of employers to provide the appropriate facilities or financial resources for retraining. In Spain, the shortage of specialists has given rise to a sort of vicious circle with regard to professional training: in a stopgap approach to the problem, training merely involves an adaptation to new functions, without regard to wider considerations; such an approach does nothing to increase the supply of manpower and indeed merely serves to exacerbate the shortage.

The demand for continuing training focuses both on technical aspects and working methods. As far as the former is concerned, employers' needs centre on operating systems, networks, fourth and fifth generation languages and artificial intelligence. Yet another area of demand for training relates to the installation of systems, organizational and management techniques and human resource management - aspects which the Danish report refers to as "soft skills".

Generally speaking, the need for continuing training itself gives rise to a market for training, and, in so doing, creates openings for manufacturers and service companies. Public institutions with responsibility for vocational training are also likely to improve their position as a result of this new demand.

4. GOVERNMENT POLICIES

Strengthening the education system

As far as jobs are concerned, government policies focus far more on supply than demand. In most Member States, government intervention has taken the form of improved planning with regard to teaching resources, in an attempt to increase the number of computer graduates and extend the range of qualifications available.

In the F.R. of Germany, Spain, France, UK, Greece, Ireland and the Netherlands medium-term government plans provide for an increase in training capacity, both in universities and other higher education establishments. In Belgium, the most dramatic initiatives have been taken in the sphere of vocational training, whilst in Denmark new computing courses have been introduced over the past five years, particularly in such areas as organization and management.

None of these moves to improve training facilities for computer specialists are easy to implement. In the short term, they have to contend with governments attempts to control or reduce public spending and even, as in Germany and the Netherlands, a shortage of qualified teaching staff. In the medium term, care must be taken to avoid saturating the job market, since the authorities would inevitably be blamed for such a development.

A marginal role for employment agencies

National or regional employment agencies do not play a major role in the job market for computer specialists in any of the Member States; the bulk of job applications and advertisements are notified by private recruitment firms, newspaper or employee associations.

The one area in which public bodies are involved is the organization of vocational training, particularly in the case of young unemployed people or unemployed workers seeking retraining. In United the Kingdom, for example, the Manpower Services Commission has introduced a whole series of vocational training facilities for young people and the unemployed - to the undoubted benefit of the employment situation.

5. PROFESSIONAL ASSOCIATIONS AND INDUSTRIAL RELATIONS

A wide range of professional associations

Professional associations for computer specialists exist in all the Member States. At an international level, they all form part of the IFIP (International Federation for Information Processing), which is actively concerned with scientific matters, including the socio-economic implications of computer development.

At national level, these associations have very little impact on industrial relations and, consequently, on the job market. Their main activities involve organising scientific conferences and, sometimes, representing computer specialists on the various advisory committees on technical standards for networks and systems. At best, they act as educational and training advisers to the public authorities, as is the case in Germany and the Netherlands. The case of the British Computer Society, which plays an active role in vocational training in the UK, must be regarded as exceptional.

A fragmented approach to trade-union membership

Denmark, with two representative bodies and around 60% of its computer specialists in trade unions, constitutes a notable exception in an industry where generally low trade-union membership is reinforced by the dim view of such membership among more highly qualified executives and technicians taken by certain large transnational companies.

The most widespread form of trade-union membership involves employee or executive unions in sectors where the latter unions already have a firm foothold, that is existing organizations rather than unions which have been specially created for computer specialists. This is particularly true in Germany, Belgium, France and the UK; although the precise figures for trade-union membership are not known, they are reputedly low in comparison with those for other executives and white-collar workers. In Ireland, two executive and technicians' unions (ASTMS and TASS) created a common body in February 1988 with a view to organizing computer specialists. Known as the MSF, this new organization is already recognized as a legitimate negotiator with both employers and the public authorities. Now firmly established, the creation of the MSF means that Ireland currently ranks alongside Denmark as an exception which confirm the rule.

Given the current situation in which the job market is dominated by supply, salaries are negotiated individually, mobility is high and trade-union membership low, it is hardly surprising that there are no specific collective agreements for computer professionals. The latter are affected by agreements of this sort only when classified as "executives".

In search of a code of professional ethics...

Ever since the abortive attempt made by the Council of Europe in 1977, there have been no further proposals for a supranational code of ethics. Most of the national professional associations approached the question of professional ethics either from the standpoint of the responsibility of computer specialists for the protection of individual freedoms or from that of the problems of computer fraud and software copyright. The few codes of professional conduct which exist - for exemple, in the UK and the Netherlands - are not legally binding and merely offer general guidelines on good professional practice.

The issue of social responsibility among computer specialists is quite a different matter. Germany and France have witnessed the emergence of associations whose specific aim is to raise awareness among computer specialists with regard to such matters as employment, freedom, peace and development. They appear to attract a large audience, on a par with the "computers and society" section of the IFIP.

...or a professional identity?

As the Belgian report points out, the attempt to define a code of professional ethics is fraught with difficulties, since computer professionals do not exhibit to any of the characteristics associated with other protected professions (doctors, lawyers, architects, for example). They must, therefore, look elsewhere in seeking to establish their professional identity.

As will be seen from the twelve national reports, the quest for professional identity now centres on relations with users, the extent of the division of labour among the various professions, the balance between technical and organizational skills and the links between training and employment. These variables also happen to be the most significant factors in the development of the job market for computer professionals.

Gérard VALENDUC
November 1988

BELGIUM

Gérard VALENDUC
Labour-University Foundation
Brussels

1. DEFINING "COMPUTER PROFESSIONALS"

In Belgium there is no single accepted definition of the term "computer professionals". Three different definitions can be given based either on to the degrees awarded, the functions identified within firms or the classification of professions in the light of job applications.

As far as degrees are concerned, there are two types of computer professionals: **graduates in computer studies** (2 years) who have attended a non-university higher-education establishment, and information-technology **engineers** (5 years) and **bachelors** (4 years) or masters (5 years) of computer science, who have received a university education. The latter group also includes university graduates in other disciplines who choose to supplement their education with a special qualification in computing (1 year), and even business-studies, administration or management graduates who take computer science as an option. In addition, improvement courses (evening or weekend classes) lead to qualifications of an equivalent level to short higher-education courses (**programmers, computer** technicians) and technical secondary education (computer **operator**).

Another definition can be derived from the categories used in the surveys conducted every five years by SOBEMAP(1) and the survey carried out in 1984 by the EURODATUM consultancy on behalf of the professional association ASAB/VEBI(2). These classifications appear in Table I. Both EURODATUM and SOBEMAP list functions as opposed to professions.

---

(1) SOBEMAP, Ordiscopie 1977, 1982, 1987.

(2) EURODATUM, Computers in Belgian firms: computerized and "computerizable" establishments, Study compiled for, and published by, ASAB/VABI, Brussels, 1984.

The placement departments of the National Office of Employment (NOE) are alone in having devised a systematic classification of computing occupations. This classification (Table 1) comprises 28 headings and provides a detailed description of each profession(3).

It is, however, rarely employed: the NOE merely uses it for the collection and computerized processing of information on job seekers and company vacancies, and not for the publication of unemployment statistics, which cover all the various computer-related professions together. Nor is it used by any other public body for the purpose of identifying existing jobs.

---

(3) NOE, Systematic classification according to professions, Code 0-96 "Data processors and other allied professions - informatici en andere aanverwante beroepen". National Office of Employment, Brussels.

Table 1: Correlations between definitions of professions

NOE	EURODATUM	SOBEMAP
computer manager computer manager data manager	computer manager	
software engineer systems engineer network architect data-base designer		system analyst
computer project manager	project manager	
systems analyst program analyst analyst/programmer	analysts	analysts
application programmer systems programmer technical back-up, and development staff	programmers	programmers
data manager data-processing auditor network manager computer-room manager preparatory-work computer console operator operator	operating staff	operating staff
general maintenance engineer maintenance engineer (Soft) maintenance engineer (Hard) remote maintenance engineer		customer service
data-processing correspondent other data-processing staff	correspondent	

2. MAIN CHARACTERISTICS OF THE JOB MARKET

Quantitative information on the market for computer professionals is scarce and tends to be fairly disparate. Concerned by the chronic lack of statistics, the Central Economic Council and the National Labour Council issued reports in 1984 and 1987 calling for a better statistical study of qualifications associated with the new information technologies(4).

2.1 Output of the education system

One of the primary sources of manpower is provided by computer science graduates leaving full-time education; in the course of the last five years (1982 - 1986), the number of university graduates specialising in computing tripled, whilst the total number of graduates increased by 30%.

More specifically, the number of computer-science graduates has tended to level off since 1984, following a period of rapid growth in the early 80s. The number of diplomas awarded under improvement courses quadrupled between 1982 and 1986, thus indicating a need for retraining among the younger working population. As far as university degrees are concerned, there has been a marked increase both in the number of specialized degrees (degrees in computing), and in the number of complementary degrees obtained either in conjunction, with or upon completion of, another degree course. The latter example points to the growing popularity of "dual qualifications" - a phenomenon which is not confined to the computer industry.

Another significant manpower source is the vocational training provided by the National Office of Employment (NOE), for the benefit both of the unemployed and the employed. Since 1982, this particular function of the National Office of Employment has, along with the whole area of vocational training, been the responsibility of the departments for the Flemish and French speaking Communities.

Except in the case of specific vocational training for programmers and analysts, the NOE general computing courses provide training in the use of the latest software packages: word processing, spreadsheets, data-base management.

---

(4) EEC, Report on the need for data and quantitative and qualitative research relating to the economic and social effects of information technology, Central Council for the Economy and National Labour Council, 28 June 1984. Report on the compilation of statistical data in matters of information technology, Central Council for the Economy, 2 October 1987.

The number of successfully completed computer training courses (i.e. resulting in the award of the National Office of Employment certificate) increased by 70% between 1983 and 1986; in 1986, this corresponded to 22% of the total number of trainees, as against 19% in 1983(5).

Alongside the various state education establishments (schools and universities) and vocational-training facilities (NOE), there are several private sources of training. This is mainly offered by sectoral vocational-training centres set up by employers' federations, private secretarial and accountancy colleges, continuing adult-education associations and computer manufacturers and consultants, prepared to play a role in organising a market for training. Some manufacturers (particularly IBM and SIEMENS) have collaborated with the National Office of Employment and are now actively engaged in training job seekers before placing them in employment.

2.2 Computer jobs within firms

The EURODATUM study(6) provides the most comprehensive source of information on the distribution of computer professionals among the various sectors of the economy. That survey partially overlaps with the IRES/INCAP study(7) conducted in the same year within the framework of a research programme funded by the Scientific Policy Programming Departments.

Table II shows that the first five sectors (in descending order: business services, retailing, Civil Service departments, banking and insurance, metal manufacture) account for three-quarters of all computer professionals; 68% of these specialists are employed in the services sector, as opposed to 29% in industry.

---

(5) NOE, Annual reports, 1982, 1983, 1984, 1985, 1986.

(6) EURODATUM, op. cit. pp 76, 77 and 94.

(7) Crott R., Houard J., Claes P., De Bondt R., Sleuwagen L;, Information, computer and telecommunication activities: statistical indicators for Belgium, Scientific Policy Programming Depertments,Brussels, 1987; this study reproduces and analyses the results of the IRES/INCAP survey.

According to the EURODATUM report, the breakdown of the various professions is as follows:
- data-processing manager   12%
- project manager   8%
- analyst   15%
- programmer   20%
- operating staff   37%
- trainee   4%
- data-processing correspondent   4%

IRES/INCAP and EURODATUM estimated that computer professionals accounted for 2.8% and 3.9% respectively of total company workforce in 1984.

Table II: Employment figures for computer professionals (1984) according to economic sectors (NACE)

NACE	Sector	DPM	PM	A	P	OS	T	DPC	Tot
0	Agriculture	18	18	0	18	90	0	0	144
1,21-23	Energy, water, mining	209	100	632	1061	927	64	57	3050
24-26	Chemicals, glass, plastics	532	385	755	796	1199	281	284	4232
3	Metal manufacture	1010	564	698	1080	3070	268	258	6948
41-42	Food indust.	363	183	401	498	925	23	270	2663
43-45	Textile, leather clothing	335	162	256	454	992	36	11	2246
47	Printing, publishing	335	144	268	268	702	18	0	1735
46,48,49	Other processing indust.	471	144	225	468	983	36	36	2363
5	Building, Civil Engin.	311	131	52	221	649	77	18	1459
61-65	Retailing	1752	619	1164	1330	5390	252	360	10867
66-67	Hotel/Catering, Repairs	54	0	18	0	198	0	0	270
7	Transport, Commun.	313	157	201	340	1360	134	150	2655
81-82	Banking, Insur.	745	804	1399	2438	3392	291	761	9830
83-85	Business services	1739	1976	3555	4039	3504	511	638	15962
91-94	Civil service, teaching	1009	608	1327	1767	4270	675	401	10057
95-99	Other departments	396	364	595	1317	2109	187	18	4986
???	Unspecified	108	0	54	18	144	0	0	324
1-4	Industries	3255	1682	3235	4625	8798	726	916	23237
6-9	Services	6008	4528	8259	11231	20223	2050	2328	54627
0-9	Total	9700	6359	11600	16113	29904	2853	3262	79791

DPM = Data-processing Manager
PM = Project Manager
A = Analyst
P = Programmer
OS = Operating staff
T = Trainee
DPC = Data-processing correspondent
TOT = Total number of computer specialists

Source: EURODATUM - ASAB/VEBI survey, FTU statistics.

The latest available information on the **breakdown of computer jobs according to qualifications** is contained in the general population census of 1981, which was published by the National Institute of Statistics (NIS) in 1986(8). The NIS classifies computer specialists in three categories:

- data processors and system analysts
- computer programmers and engineers
- operating or data-entry staff

---

(8) NIS, Census of the population on 1.3.1981: school population and educational level, Report issued by the National Institute of Statistics, n 4, 1986.

Holders of a university degree or other higher education diploma tend to work as data processors and analysts rather than as processing or data-entry operators. However, more than a third of data processors and nearly half of the programmers were not educated beyond secondary level, where there is no diploma in computing. This fact highlights the importance of in-house company training and reveals the highly flexible nature of the link between initial training and employment.

The correlation between qualifications and job status is therefore clear: a high level of initial training may ensure access to the most highly skilled jobs but the latter are not the exclusive preserve of highly qualified graduates.

2.3 Manpower supply and demand

Just what sort of qualifications are firms looking for? Few studies have been published on the demand for computer professionals on the job market. A few items of information can be gleaned from a study conducted by the Information Department on Education and the Professions(9). In 1983, according to this report, 51% of vacancies were for analysts and programming staff, 12% for operating staff, 9% for research or project managers, 13% for systems specialists and, 8% for commercial staff.

There is little available information on growth rates in the various professions. The authors of the IBM study(10) refer to an ECSA survey (European Computer Services Association), published in 1983, which estimated the annual growth rates in demand for computing jobs in Belgium as follows:
- operating and data-entry staff   - 1.3%
- analysts and programmers   + 4.9%
- sales and marketing   + 4.6%
- other computer staff   + 4.1%

Given the above-mentioned growth rates, demand for computer professionals should be some where between 2 000 and 2 500 specialists per year (analysts, programmers and other computer staff); university and other higher-education graduates account for fewer than 2 000 of these specialists per year.

---

(9) Coppe F., <u>Computers: professions, training,</u> SIEP, Brussels, pp 28-30.

(10) De Bondt R., et al., <u>Computer Industry in Belgium,</u>
 IBM-Belgium, 1986, p 46.

In its statistical records on the number of job-seekers in each profession, the National Office of Employment has only kept maintained a separate "computing" file covering encompasses all the professions listed in the detailed NOE classification since 1987. During this brief period, the only significant developments were a slight decrease in the number of unemployed receiving benefits (-4.6%) and a slight increase in the number of job-seekers, particularly part-time workers seeking full-time employment.

2.4 Adjustment and regulating mechanisms on the job market

It is not possible to formulate a coherent, overall view of the job market for computer professionals on the basis of the information available. As LOBET-MARIS points out, the absence of a reliable study of the job market has given rise to a so-called **"market in different perceptions of the job market"**(11) in Belgium. This notion underlies the following description of the two main mechanisms which serve to govern and regulate the job market, namely salaries and company **recruitment strategies**.

When it comes to setting salary levels for highly qualified computer staff, employers can refer to the various multi-client surveys conducted by specialist consultants to which access is strictly limited.

According to SOBEMAP, the proportion of firms' overall computer budgets earmarked for research and development staff (software) has remained stable over the past ten years, whereas the proportion of funds allocated to operating staff has considerably decreased.

The average monthly salary of research and development staff ranges from BF 83 000 to BF 124 000 per month, depending on the size of the firm concerned and the extent to which it has been computerized. These average figures conceal other disparities linked to the educational qualifications of R&D staff; within this very broad category, the salaries paid to designers are continually increasing whereas salary levels among analysts and programmers seem to have levelled off. In Belgium, highly-qualified marketing staff are still in shortest supply and it is in this category that salary brackets tend to be widest.

---

(11) Lobet-Maris C., The link between training and employment and firms' strategies, in the Computer Journal, No. 7, October 1987, p 22.

Finally, it is clear that employers are anxious to find a more stable mechanism for regulating the job market than that offered by salary fluctuations, linked to "peaks" in demand or the vagaries of fashion. Two employers' associations - INSEA (federation of computer service firms) and ABCI (the Belgian Association of Computer Manufacturers) - are currently engaged in to the search for a more abstract regulating mechanism. A multi-sector working group was set up in 1987 for precisely this purpose. If this "cartelization" of the job market becomes established, smaller service companies, for whom above-average salaries are the only reliable way of attracting high-calibre staff, will continue to cause problems in this area.

Where **company strategies** are concerned, it should be borne in mind that two job markets exist for computer specialists: the external market and the in-house company market based on mobility and continuing training. Claire LOBET-MARIS[12] attempts to pinpoint these strategies by examining firms' relationship to the job market. She identifies two opposing groups, separated by a range of intermediate positions: companies "dominated" by, and those seeking to dominate, the job market.

Within the **"dominated"** category, the search for highly qualified computer staff is conducted directly on the external job market; direct competition with other firms compels these companies to attract highly qualified staff by offering exceptional incentives which go far beyond the provisions of existing agreements and sectoral rates. The introduction of contracts and special service regulations, however, tends to produce an imbalance in the running of these firms, with the result that some have converted their computer departments into independent profit-making centres or even subsidiaries.

The **"dominant"** firms pursue the opposite strategy, seeking to maintain a certain degree of uniformity with regard to service regulations in order to combat soaring salaries, internal imbalances or a highly compartmentalized approach to job functions. Such firms are primarily looking for young graduates, with high general qualifications who can be trained in computing. Once recruited, these graduates work both within the field of computing and in other company departments, according to the rules of mobility applicable to all executives. Naturally, this strategy requires extensive training facilities. As far as salaries are concerned, computer specialists enjoy similar conditions to other executives. When determining their basic salary, however, no employer can afford to ignore the prevailing situation on the job market. Various methods of calculation have therefore been developed in an attempt to fix the so-called "abstract" salary component, which at times can represent to between 15 and 20% of the official scale.

---

(12) Lobet-Maris C., The link between training and employment and company strategies, op. cit. p 20.

2.5 Case studies

The **software industry** is one of the very few sectors of the economy where more detailed information on the job market for computer professionals is available. Overall employment in these companies is increasing at a constant rate of nearly 10% per year and turnover rose by an average of 16% between 1973 and 1983. The breakdown of the various computer-related professions in software companies shows a clear preponderance of consultants and analysts (two-thirds of all jobs) over programmers. There is a strong correlation between programming jobs and computer-science degrees; in the case of jobs involving design and analysis, university graduates occupy more than 80% of all posts. Since 1985, there has been a slowdown in the increase in salaries paid to programmers and analysts; only the average salary levels for senior staff continue to improve.

In Belgium, **computer manufacturers** deal exclusively with sales and maintenance. According to COPPE[13], they are interested in five main types of employee: systems analysts, analysts, salesmen, technical-commercial assistants and maintenance engineers.

In the **banking sector**, it would appear that the sort of computer staff required depends largely on the organizational structure of the bank concerned. The re-orientation of computer projects in line with the banking services offered, creates a need for employees who can combine "technical" with "financial" skills; for this reason, recruitment officers have gradually begun to show a preference for combined qualifications over highly specialised skills[14].

---

[13] Coppe F., <u>Computing: profession, training,</u> op. cit., pp 10-14.

[14] Eraly A., <u>Computing as an organisational problem,</u> in Wilkin L., <u>Computing and organisations,</u> ULB Brussels, 1986.

3. SOCIAL ASPECTS OF THE DEVELOPMENT OF THE COMPUTER PROFESSIONS

3.1 Changes in duties and qualifications

Computing professions would appear to be in a constant state of flux. Closer examination of this instability shows it to be the product of a dual, apparently contradictory phenomenon: **job content** is changing very rapidly while **employment structures** remain the same.

The few studies or articles seeking to identify the changing **content** of computer jobs reveal no decisive trends. Four main changes can, however, be indicated:

- certain functions which, until recently, were the preserve of trained computer specialists, are becoming more commonplace and are being increasingly taken over by users;

- the procedure for integrating computer-related functions within companies is changing rapidly; the computer department, which was initially conceived as a logistical tool outside the existing hierarchy, has been split into a number of "computer units" within other departments; only the operating and systems functions remain centralized;

- the tendency of computer staff to specialized in different applications has led to the gradual emergence of a new sort of data processor combining "general" computer skills with "specialist" knowledge in a particular area of application;

- the modernization of tools and working methods among computer specialists means that computer-related tasks are becoming increasingly automated, while employers are demanding ever higher qualification levels, particularly where the development of networks and operating systems is concerned.

Faced with these rapid changes in job content, **employment structures** have remained fairly stable, and the following four main job categories can still be distinguished[15]: operating, applications, systems, sales and marketing (only in the case of manufacturers and software companies).

---

(15) Lobet-Maris C., Data processors: from artisan to office worker: the challenge of change, in Data Processors, University Press, 1986; pp 367-391.

The relative stability of employment structures is clearly illustrated by the **"life-cycle of qualifications"**; within the space of a few years, most new qualifications are absorbed into existing professions in three main phases:

- <u>the appearance</u> of a new, specialized qualification and a cyclical shortage of specialists on the job market;
- <u>standardization</u> and harmonization, due both to the spread of new technology and the dissemination of knowledge throughout the education and training system;
- <u>the absorption</u> of new functions, once fully established, within existing professions, subject to slight adaptation or re-orientation of the latter.

The balance between stable employment structures and changing job contents must be struck within firms themselves through their **organizational policy**. Some authors, such as ERALY(16), believe that this whole issue has a crucial bearing on the future of computer specialists. The importance of organizational choices for the definition of computer tasks was also highlighted by BAISIER(17), in a study of the extent to which employees are informed and consulted during the successive stages of developing and implementing a computer project.

3.2 Changes in service regulations and careers

The issue of **professional mobility** is not restricted to the higher echelons of computer-related professions. According to SOBEMAP, the average turnover rate is 12% in the case of computer professionals employed by manufacturers, with significant variations between firms. In user firms, the overall average turnover is 7.2%, rising to 9.5% in the case of research and design staff and 9.3% in the case of operating staff. Turnover is highest, however, among data-entry staff: 13.7%(18).

The **status** enjoyed by computer specialists depends both on their qualifications and on firms' recruitment strategies.

---

(16) Eraly A., op. cit. p 25.

(17) Albertijn M., Baisier L., Wijgaerts D., <u>Informatie en overleg bij technologie-introducties,</u> Stichting Technologie Vlaanderen, SERV, Antwerp, May 1987.

(18) Simi H., <u>Data processors play leapfrog,</u> Trends/Tendances 9.04.87.

In the lower professional categories, there are few exceptions to the conventional service regulations. In the more senior professional categories, the spectrum widens to cover two extremes: on the one hand, employment contracts and salary levels negotiated individually between employers and computer specialists, in accordance with the various reference scales compiled by consultants and, on the other hand, the contracts, salaries and regulations appropriate to senior executives, subject to certain modifications.

3.3 The link between training and employment

The general trend is as follows: in the case of <u>programmers,</u> a **definite** link can be established between training and employment while, in the case of <u>analysts, designers and consultants,</u> such a link **no longer exists**. This observation is based both on analysis of the available information and companies' training policies.

The link between a university degree and programming jobs is now well-established, although the medium-term future is uncertain. Today's graduates find themselves sandwiched between two developments: the increasing readiness of analysts to assume responsibility for entire projects, and, the expansion of the software packages market, which allows firms to become computerized without having to develop their own programs.

As far as analysts and consultants are concerned, the link between training and employment is much more flexible. There is a clear connection between such jobs and the <u>level</u> of training received since the profession is dominated by university graduates. The professionals in question, however, are not necessarily computer-science graduates, since firms' tend to recruit graduates from a range of disciplines to fill these posts.

4. GOVERNMENT POLICIES

4.1 Policies with regard to computer education and training

These have been no recent policy measures relating to the training of computer specialists. The State has sometimes been slow to modify its recruitment criteria in order to recognize computer graduates in spite of their "valid" qualifications. At secondary school level, decrees issued by the Departments for the French- and Flemish-speaking Communities have made introductory computer courses a compulsory part of the general curriculum since 1986.

As far as **vocational training** is concerned, both Communities have taken steps to introduce new technology into the programmes offered by the NOE. Computer training centres are either run directly by the NOE, or mixed centres set up in 1986 in conjuction with firms, private associations or other civil service departments. In 1985, the increase in the number of trainees enrolled in computer courses prompted the NOE's National Training and Pedagogical Studies Centre to institute courses aimed at training teachers in operating systems, office software packages and CAD/CAM systems. Overall, the effect of a joint, Community-based approach to training has greatly increased the NOE's capacity for innovation, and computer training courses have been among the first to benefit.

4.2 Policies relating to the recruitment and service regulations of computer professionals in the public sector

In civil service departments and semi-public institutions which are not classified as public enterprises, the **service regulations of computer specialists** are laid down in the Royal Decree of 3 December 1969, which has successfully resisted all attempts at change for nearly twenty years, in spite of the fact that the job descriptions it contains have become obsolete.

The "BODART report"[19] confirms that the tasks performed by operators and programmers now call for higher qualifications than those stipulated in the Decree, and that computer professionals require further definition so as to cover, for example, project managers, data managers, network managers and systems engineers.

---

[19] Bodart F., The efficient use of information technology by the authorities, Report to the Minister for the Civil Service, INBEL, Brussels, 1984.

The rigid and archaic nature of the existing legal provisions seriously affects the careers of computer professionals in the civil service who are subject to **recruitment problems**, lower average salaries than in the private sector, limited promotion prospects and limited mobility.

It is interesting to compare this lack of flexibility in respect of service regulations and recruitment with the dynamic training initiatives launced by the Civil Service Ministry (DGSF) since 1985. The **training initiatives** in question relate to the formulation and monitoring of overall data-processing plans, the position of data-processing correspondent and the retraining of computer staff already working in the civil service.

5. PROFESSIONAL ASSOCIATIONS AND INDUSTRIAL RELATIONS

5.1 Professional associations

In Belgium, there are currently about ten professional associations for computer specialists, the majority of which belong to the "Belgian Federation of Computer Specialist Associations" (BFCSA), which represents them at an international level. With two exceptions, the Belgian Association of Telecommunication Users (ABUT) and the Informatic Services Association (INSEA), the member associations of the BFCSA cannot be said to play an active public role, insofar as they do not engage in politics or concern themselves with industrial relations.

The ABUT acts as a spokesman for approximately two hundred firms which are major telecommunications users. Its task is to defend their interests in relation to the authorities and the post and telecommunications service (RTT) and within European users' associations. ABUT is in favour of deregulating telecommunications and telematics services in Belgium.

INSEA is an employers' association which represents software companies; in this capacity, it is also a member of FABRIMETAL, which is the metal-manufacturing industry's employers' association. INSEA openly supports the development of computer services in Belgium calling, in particular, for a public procurement policy in the sphere of software packages. In addition, INSEA advises its members on recruitment and salary policy with regard to computer professionals.

5.2 Trade unions and computer professionals

Belgian trade unions have no specific structure for the organizaton of computer professionals. Depending on their status, employees are classified either as "employees" or "executives". There is no available information on trade-union membership among computer specialists. Employees appear to join unions in firms whit a strong tradition of trade-union membership among executives and skilled office workers, as is the case, for example, in banking, insurance and the public sector. Given this state of affairs, it is hardly surprising that trade unions do not make specific demands on behalf of computer specialists.

5.3 Collective agreements

There is no Collective Work Agreement specifically aimed at people in the computer industry, either at national or sectoral level. Computer professionals are specifically included in collective agreements which determine job classification and conditions of employment only where they are classified as "executives" and subject to executive service regulations.

5.4 Computer specialists and new forms of social relations

The collections published by BERLEUR et al.(20) and WILKIN(21) describe a number of attempts by Belgian firms to introduce worker participation. The cases quoted reveal that a key factor for the computer-related professions is the development of relations with users, via such new mechanisms as the creation of user groups or increased user participation. Such initiatives, however, remain isolated.

5.5 Professional ethics (deontology)

There is no code of ethics for computer specialists in Belgium. In the Seventies, two professional associations, the FAIB and the ASAB/VEBI, attempted, unsuccessfully, to draw up a code of ethics.

At a more basic level, it seems reasonable to ask, like LACROSSE(22), whether the notion of a "professional model" really applies to the computer industry. The issue of the professional identity of computer professionals has long been a subject of debate, since many professional associations had the initial task of attempting to formulate a code of professional ethics.

---

(20) Berleur J., Lobet-Maris C., Poswick R.F., Valenduc G., van Bastelaer Ph., <u>Data processors: computer specialists in their relations with users,</u> University Press of Namur, 1986.

(21) Wilkin L., <u>Computing and organisations,</u> Published by Brussels University, 1986.

(22) Lacrosse J.M. <u>Is there a future for the professional model in computing?</u> Computer Journal, n 7, October 1987

These attempts invariably failed, since the data processing profession does not meet any of the criteria normally used to define protected professions: neither <u>cognitive</u> criteria, involving the accumulation of a body of knowledge unavailable to the uninitiated, nor <u>normative</u> criteria based on professional ethics and self-regulation, nor criteria linked to <u>professional practice</u> monitored by professional associations, specific teaching bodies and ethical codes apply in the case of computer professionals.

The notion of "professionalization" cannot therefore be understood in the sense of the construction of a "professional model". All of which lends weight to the argument that any attempt to form an overall picture of the job market for computer professionals should be based, first and foremost, on the nature of the division of labour and the forms of organizational integration adopted.

DENMARK

Niels BJORN-ANDERSEN, Finn BORUM, Margrete BROCH,
Benedicte DUE-THOMSEN, Andrew L. FRIEDMAN, Ole KUDSK,
Mette MONSTED, Jesper STRANDGÅRD PEDERSEN and Marianne RISBERG (1)
Copenhagen Business School
Frederiksberg

1. DEFINITION OF "INFORMATION TECHNOLOGY PROFESSIONALS"

In order to define an IT-professional we have to consider two criteria: (a) educational background and (b) position in the organization. The threshold level in the educational definition is put at minimum one year of computer-related education. In the occupational definition the threshold is put at the level of programmers and data-entry operators. This implies that all kinds of end-users are excluded from the definition of "IT-professionals", for example both white- and blue-collar workers using terminals, and teachers in the education system.

We have chosen the following job categories for IT professionals which, for reasons of available statistics, exclude sales and marketing IT professionals working, for example, for IT vendors (2):

- APPLICATIONS and SYSTEMS:

    Head of computing (Edb-chef), Systems manager (Edb-systemchef), Programming manager (Edb-programmeringschef), Systems consultant (System konsulent), Systems planner (Systemplanlaegger), Systems programmer (Systemprogrammør), Analyst/programmer (Edb-planlaegger/programmør), Programmer and applications programmer (Edb-programmør).

---

(1) CHIPS Project, Institute of Organization and Industrial Sociology, and Institut of Informatics and Management Accounting, Copenhagen Business School, Frederiksberg.

(2) Borum F., Risberg M. The IT-professionals: A statistical description, August 1988, Chips Working Paper no. 9

- OPERATIONS:

  Operations manager (Edb-driftschef), Operations planner (Edb-driftsplanlaegger), Operator (Edb-operatør), Data-entry supervisor (Edb-tasteoperatør leder), and Data-entry operator (Edb-tasteoperatør).

2. LABOUR MARKET

2.1 Output of the education system

The education system in Denmark for IT-professionals is almost entirely public. The only exceptions are the short courses offered by vendors and a handful of small private educational institutions. There are three main levels of education in Denmark after primary school: vocational training, short higher educations and higher education (for the latter two high school diploma are required). Only education with chief emphasis on IT subjects is described.

- <u>Vocational training</u>

  Courses for EDP-assistants are available in 10 commercial schools and lead to the occupations of programmer, operations planner, and even analyst after some professional experience. The length of courses is 1 1/2 to 2 1/2 years or 5 years as part-time studies. The courses for micro-instructors are available in three commercial schools. They last one year and lead to the occupation of maintenance and installation instructor.

- <u>Short higher education</u>

  "Datamatiker" courses have been available since 1984 in two commercial schools; they are of 2 1/2 years duration and lead to the function of analyst-programmer. The final output does not yet appear in the 1986 statistics.

- Higher education

In five Danish universities, major or minor combinations in computer sciences or computer engineering lead to the higher-level occupations of analyst-programmer, system programmer, system consultant, instructor and research worker. The studies are 4 1/2 to 5 1/2 years duration. Degrees in computer engineering are also conferred by some technical colleges. A second possible course of study at university level leads to IT degrees through business, economics or administration master degrees. These degrees lead to software-oriented occupations, systems design, application design, user and customer services.

The following table provides some data concerning the annual and cumulated output of the education system.

Education level	Year of establishment	Yearly output	Total output till 1986
Vocational training			
EDP assistant	1972	750	5 000
Micro-instructor	1982	15	40
Short higher education			
Datamatiker	1984	100	0
Higher education			
Combination Computer Sc.	1972	140	1 000
Computer engineer		40	150
Business & Computer Sc.	1983/85	300	50
Total		1 345	6 240

As can be seen from this description, the primary source of educated IT professionals has been and still is the EDP-assistant course. Approximately 5 000 of the 6 300 IT professionals trained up to 1986 are EDP-assistants and approx. 750 of 1 345 IT professionals trained each year are EDP-assistants.

Public post-graduate course in IT subjects is not highly developed in Denmark. Most important is the "DATANOM" course which is primarily available as post-graduate course for EDP-assistants. The second major possibility is the Bachelor of Commerce in Informatics which is taken mainly by EDP-assistants or engineers and other academics as their second degree.

2.2 The labour market for IT-professionals.

The Danish Statistical Bureau (DS) produces an annual statistic on private-sector employees, based upon data from employers on job titles, salaries, age, sex, education, etc. This has been produced in its present form since 1982, based upon data from the previous year.

The sample for 1981 covered 56 % of all private-sector white-collar workers while in 1986 the sample increased to 68 %. In 1987 the coverage was 70 %. BORUM AND RISBERG (1988) adjusted the figures in order to get a 100 % estimate of the IT-population [3]:

	1981	1986	1987
DS-figures	7 093 (56%)	12 869 (68%)	13 852 (70%)
Corrected figures	12 666 (100%)	18 925 (100%)	19 789 (100%)

---

[3] Borum F., Risberg M. (1988), op.cit. and DS, <u>Løn- og indkomststatestik</u>, 1988/1

Based on these figures, the number of IT-professionals in 1986 can be estimated at around 20 000, approx 0.8 % of the total labour force. However, we believe that the number is between 25 000 and 30 000 especially taking into account that employees in small organizations are left out of the official statistics, and that many sales/marketing people working for IT-companies are not included in the official statistics. One reason why the number of IT-professionals is no longer increasing is the fact that the borderline between IT-professionals and users is becoming blurred. This is to a large extent due to the introduction of fourth-generation tools which allow "non-IT-professionals" to carry out "traditional" IT jobs.

The official DS statistics, which account only for a proportion of all IT-professionals as mentioned above, show that a majority, 76 % in 1986, of IT-professionals are men, as can be seen in the figure. It is especially noteworthy that there are relatively more women in the lower-paid jobs within operations. However, one should note that the number of women top managerial levels is increasing (4).

---

(4) DS, Løn- og indkomststatestik, 1982/1 and 1987/1, and Borum and Risberg, 1988, op.cit.

	1981		1986	
	male	female	male	female
head of computing	291	16	493	75
systems manager	156	2	224	13
programming manager	89	3	117	3
systems consultant	403	60	1 558	358
systems planner	1 062	142	1 225	286
systems programmer	476	30	904	97
analyst/programmer	(a)	(a)	966	318
programmer	1 172	294	1 701	560
Total applications and systems	3 649 / 87%	547 / 13%	7 188 / 81%	1 710 / 19%
operations manager	73	6	195	20
operations planner	358	34	545	106
operator	992	170	1 702	412
data entry supervisor	18	124	29	87
data entry operator	52	1 070	69	806
Total operations	1 493 / 52%	1 404 / 48%	2 540 / 64%	1 431 / 36%
Total	5 142 / 73%	1 951 / 27%	9 728 / 76%	3 141 / 24%

(a) Does not appear in the statistics this year.

When it comes to age, IT-professionals are young, as shown in the following figure, which shows the age distribution of IT-professionals and white collar employees in %, in 1986 (5):

Age	IT-professionals	all white collar	difference
- 24	12	13	- 1
25 - 29	23	16	+ 7
30 - 34	22	15	+ 7
35 - 39	18	15	+ 3
40 - 44	14	15	- 1
45 - 49	5	10	- 5
50 -	5	16	- 11

As to geographic distribution, 61 % of all IT-professionals are employed in the Copenhagen area.

In general, the employment situation for IT-professionals is excellent, even though the two unions, PROSA and SAM-DATA/HK, which together organize 13 800 IT-professionals, are worried about the situation for the EDP-assistants.

2.3 Labour market regulation processes

The following figure provides a graphical representation of the correlation between average monthly income, position, and gender for individuals of the same age (6). BORUM AND RISBERG (1988) make the point that women are paid less than men in the same position and at the same age. Furthermore, the figure gives some indications of the most obvious career patterns (see section 3.1 for a discussion of career patterns).

Comparisons with other groups of employees confirm the general pattern that IT-professionals are well paid. Out of the total group of male employees, 36 % were paid higher than the average salary for the upper quartile of all male white-collar employees, 58% were better paid than the average salary, and all except data-entry operators were better paid than the lower quartile of male white-collar employees.

---

(5) Borum and Risberg, 1988, op.cit.

(6) Borum and Risberg, 1988, op.cit. p 20 and p 80

The corresponding figures for women show that only 13 % of the female IT-professionals are better paid than average male white-collar employees. However, 73 % of the female IT-people receive salaries above the upper quartile of female white-collar employees. The 27 % who come out below are the data entry operators.

3. SOCIAL ASPECTS AND TRENDS

3.1 The jobs of IT-professionals

In this section, we focus on important trends characterizing the jobs of IT professionals. More precisely, the section describes qualifications upon recruitment and upon promotion, organization of IT-jobs, working conditions, roles, career patterns, mobility patterns of IT-professionals and copyrights.

There is no single itinerary or course of education leading to computing. Therefore, the skills of the IT professionals cover a wide range of courseal backgrounds (7).

	1970	1986 (estimated)
- High Shool only	22 %	20 %
- Edp-assistant		20 %
- Bachelor in business economics (HA/HD)	3 %	5 %
- Short business courses (HH/Merkonom)	1 %	10 %
- Engineers or other technical courses	4 %	5 %
- University degree or equivalent (including computer sciences)	0 %	10 %
- Other	70 %	30 %

---

(7) Borum and Risberg, 1988, op.cit.

This table indicates that the qualification level within the IT-field has been rising. The most significant trend has been towards a combination of Studentereksamen (high school exam) and, subsequently, EDP-assistant. Furthermore, the ratio of academics has also been increasing. The proportion of "other courseal background" has decreased as the general eductional level in society has risen and IT have been introduced. Over the years a significantly higher number of IT-professoinals have been acquiring formal qualifications.

Since the introduction of computerization, researchers have often voiced the "deskilling hypothesis", i.e. that IT-specialists would also in due course be victims of a vertical and horizontal specialization. The development in Denmark so far shows that the opposite has occurred. IT-professionals in general still enjoy a flexible division of work, a high degree of autonomy and good career opportunities.

This is supported by FRIEDMAN (8), who reports that in the ICON survey organization structures which separate analysts and programmers were least common in Scandinavia (4-12 %) among the participating countries and most common in the United Kingdom and Japan, (36 %). Furthermore the ICON survey shows that distinguishing between analysts and programmers as separate jobs was most common in England (72 %), while the figure was as low as 40% in Denmark. In line with these data, organization structures where one person concentrates on conceptual aspects of programming activities, the so-called chief programmer teams, were not found in Denmark in the ICON survey.

BANSLER (9) argues that the reason why deskilling has not had such a profound impact in Denmark is the large proportion of small companies and the relatively high level of unionization.

---

(8) Friedman A., Understanding the employment Position of Computer programmers: a managerial strategics approach, October, 1987, CHIPS Working Paper no. 8

(9) Bansler J., Edb-faget industrialiseres - fanden tager de sidste, in Lund-Larsen M., "EDB-fagets fremtid", PROBOG 1986

Within the operations departments a great deal of automation is taking place, which is significantly reducing the need for operators and requires a change in their qualifications. It is especially the tasks around tape-stations and printer-services which will change and even significantly decrease. Another consequence is that new systems will minimize the amount of evening- and night work, so that operations will become like most other day-time jobs. The remaining tasks will probably be reduced to control and surveillance, according to CHRISTENSEN (10).

Concerning working conditions, one of the largest software houses in Denmark, KOMMUNEDATA, launched in the spring of 1988 an essay competition. The theme of the essay was the ideal future IT-job. Institutet for Fremtidsforskning (Institute for Futures Studies) has analyzed these essays (1988). Their conclusion is that authors see a post-material (post-industrial) society. The most important requirement in a job is the opportunity for self-fulfilment. The emphasis is laid on "soft/feminine" values such as social acceptance, flexibility, influence and dialogue versus the traditional "masculine values" such as performance, goal-achievement, rationality, power, and money. Furthermore, the "group", team spirit and team work will be extremely important in the future.

Not a single essayist has described her/himself as becoming a manager of other people. The role of the manager seems to change completely. The manager should not decide or be the controlling body. The manager's role is that of a "culture mediator", making sure that completely different people can work together for a common purpose. The manager must understand the employees' needs and the commitment of employees and must create an open environment which support initiatives.

The attitude of the authors to work and career is positive. Work is no longer a necessary evil to earn money. It is through work that one should find self-fulfilment. Future IT-professionals are artists, and the work place should be organized accordingly.

The final point on working conditions is that a "sperm bank" has been established where men can have their sperm deposited for ten years. The highest proportion of men using the sperm bank are computer programmers! One might guess that the reason is fear of the still unknown effects of radiation on male fertility.

---

(10) Christensen P., "Big brother" i drifts-afdelingen", in Lund-Larsen M., "EDB-fagets fremtid", PROBOG, 1986

Another key issue relates to the role of IT-professionals because the different groups in the organization, eg. top-management, middle managers and chief-users have conflicting expectations of IT-professionals. A recent comparative survey of Danish and Canadian systems developers (Bjørn-Andersen and Kumar, forthcoming) shows that Danish systems developers are more theory Y oriented than their North American counterparts. Using a second measurement, the study is comparing the relative value designers assign to three sets of systems design objectives, technical, economic and socio-political values. The score shown in the figure below illustrates the well-known fact that IT-professionals in both countries are placing most emphasis on the technical values and least emphasis on the socio-political values. However, the Danish designers place a significantly higher emphasis on the socio-political values than their North-American colleagues - almost as much as on the other two sets of values.

The following table gives an overview of Canadian and Danish value profiles guiding the development of systems:

	Technical	Economic	Socio-political
Canada	52.4	48.7	30.5
Denmark	47.1	46.2	40.3

If we look at career patterns of IT-professionals, BORUM & RISBERG (1988) noted that, for the first time in 1981, a new title, "systems consultants", appeared in the official statistics. They have two possible explanations for this phenomena: the need to create a promotion opportunity for systems analysts and the fact that implementation in the user organization is becoming more important and has led to the creation of new functions.

The most typical career patterns are shown in this figure (11):

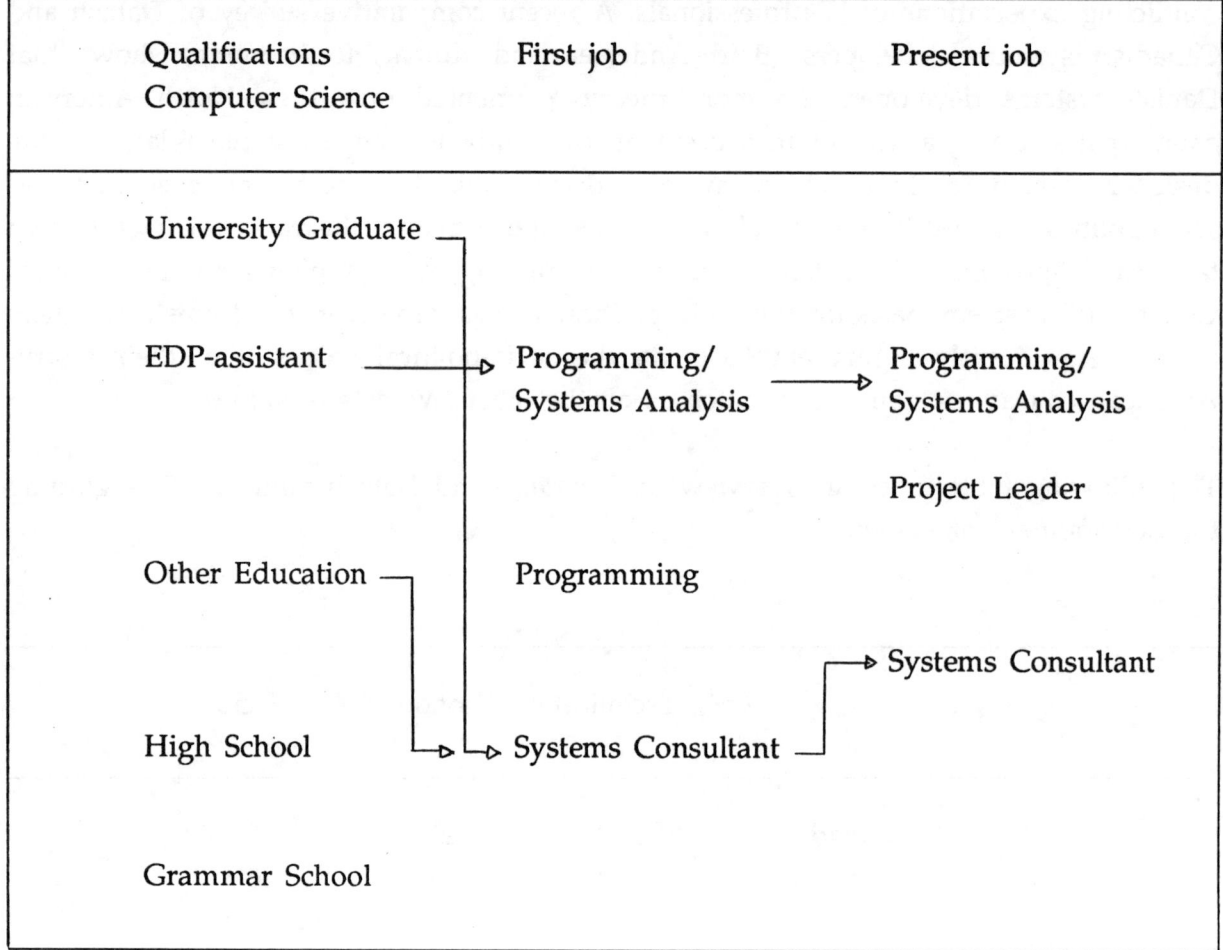

However, the IT labour market is a very open, turbulent field with rather unstructured career patterns where "the sky is the limit" irrespective of background.

---

(11) CHIPS Project, Institute of Organization and Industrial Sociology, and Institut of Informatics and Management Accounting, Copenhagen Business School, Frederiksberg.

For many years, the Danish IT labour market has been said to suffer from having high job mobility. It was said that "IT-professionals change jobs more often than they change their shirts." It is correct that labour mobility is higher for IT-professionals than for other comparable groups. This is especially true in the first few years when IT-professionals gain experience and have high expectations as to increases in salary due to high demand. However, after a few years' employment the mobility drops substantially and careers are pursued within the company instead of moving to other companies. A survey from 1977 revealed that IT-professionals had an average seniority in the company of 4-5 years (12). Today seniority is even higher.

The last issue in this section deals with the question of copyright of software. This has become a focus of attention due to the increasing dissemination and economic importance of software. There has been one case in Denmark, where programmers in Vaerdipapircentralen (Securities Central) had developed a piece of software for its own use. Later Vaerdipapircentralen sold the software to a Norwegian company for 25 million DKK. without any compensation for the employees. The employees have claimed compensation under the law of copyright, but the case has not yet been settled.

In order to remedy the situation, a new law has been proposed by The Department of Culture. According to this, all copyrights created under the conditions of employment will remain with the employer. However, the law does not cover non-permanent employees. Accordingly it is expected that if the law is passed, some of the most skilled employees will avoid employment in favour of becoming independent consultants.

3.2 Training and retraining requirements

While the major "technical" qualification needs are gradually being satisfied, all parties agree that there is a strong need for "softer qualifications", i.e. many IT-specialists need to become better skilled in communicating and understanding their users/customers, and at the same time to know more about the application areas.

In general, large companies expend large amounts of time and money on course and retraining of IT professionals, whereas the many small IT-companies place less emphasis on course. They solve their retraining problems by having a high turnover.

---

(12) Borum F., Risberg M. <u>The IT-professionals: A statistical description</u>, August 1988, Chips Working Paper no. 9

Post-graduate state education in IT subjects for IT professionals is limited to the "Datanom" course which is mainly a post-graduate course (and specialization) for EDP-assistants, and to the Bachelor of Commerce course in informatics.

A number of non-specialist IT courses, however, are offered which have substantial IT-elements, e.g. those offered by the business universities (HD) and commercial schools (merkonom) which are becoming more common among IT professionals. This underlies a trend towards more emphasis on the application areas.

Finally, another trend is towards providing training at the time it is needed. It could be called applying the "just-in-time" principle to education. The latest news in this area is to make training programs part of the systems sold to customers. The courses are then embedded in the software and can be used whenever needed.

3.3 Increasing professionalism

IT-professionals cannot be described as a professional group in the same way as doctors, lawyers etc. BJØRN-ANDERSEN & MALMVIG (1977) saw IT-professionals as a group having a "professional identity", even though only a limited number of IT-professionals were members of a professional association and few had had any formal IT-training.

Today the situation has changed substantially. 30 % of the people entering the field have had a formal training in informatics - most often as "EDP-assistants". Also, the number of academics entering the field is rising. This reflects both a societal trend and the fact that specific formal courses have been established within the IT-field. Furthermore, the unionization of IT-professionals has increased, mainly among operators and programmers.

There has been a recent change in the orientation of IT-professionals towards greater concern for IT-service customers. The prime focus has been on improving human factors and involvement of the computer users. This trend is now supplemented with a focus on service-mindedness towards the company's customers. This means that existing methods are having to undergo some changes.

Besides the associations organized within DANFIP, there are also the Danish Information Application Group (DIAG) and ESF (the association of IT-vendors). IT-vendors are in this connection a concept covering computing service companies, software houses and IT-consultants. The purpose of the association is to improve ethical and professional standards. Previously EDB-rådet played perhaps the most significant role of all IT-associations. But it was obliged to merge with Danish Dataforening a few years ago because of lack of a clear mission and lack of funds.

5.2   Unionization

Denmark has two unions dedicated exclusively to IT-profession-als: PROSA (6 800 members) and SAM-DATA/HK (7 000). PROSA is independent and SAM-DATA belongs to HK, the National Union of Clerical Workers. Besides these two, there are a number of trade oriented unions organizing almost everyone in that particular trade including IT professionals. The major examples (with the approximate numbers of IT-professionals in brackets) are the Union of Danish Bank Employees (1 600), the Union of Danish Insurance Employees (779) and DSLF, the Union of Danish Savings Bank Employees (500). Academic IT-professionals are also organized in DIF (the Union of Danish Engineers), and DJOF (the Union of Danish Law- and Economy Graduates).

Even if one considers the total estimated figure of between 25 000 and 30 000 IT-professionals, 17 000 unionized in comparison with other countries is a very high level of unionization. However, compared to the 87 % level of white-collar unionization in Denmark, it may be considered to be at a moderate level. The figure conceals marked differences between the rates of unionization in user organizations (high) and suppliers (low).

5.3   Collective agreements for IT-professionals

In the private sphere in Zealand there are mainly collective agreements within the financial sector together with some local agreements. In the private sphere the main part of the negotiations takes place on an individual basis with around 2 000 in east (Zealand) and 1 500 in the west (rest of Denmark). However, only the lowest paid IT-professionals are paid according to an agreement.

4. GOVERNMENT POLICIES

In Denmark, there are no laws or guidelines requiring specific types of training for specific jobs within the IT-field.

The only role of government in the labour market, except as a large-scale employer, is the public employment agency, Arbejdsformidlingen (AF). However, AF plays almost no role in the filling of vacancies within the IT-area. Recruitment usually takes place through advertisements in the newspapers and trade magazines. A small number of IT jobs are filled through personal contacts and some of the more senior jobs are often filled using the services of headhunting companies or private manpower selection consultants.

5. PROFESSIONAL RELATIONS

5.1 Role of professional groups and associations

There are several professional groups and associations in Denmark. Almost all of these are organized within DANFIP (Danish Federation for Information Processing) which represents Denmark in IFIP. Members of DANFIP are Danish associations that have purely professional objectives and with an interest and qualifications to participate in cooperation with IFIP.

The present member-associations are Dansk Dataforening (Danish Data Association), Dansk Selskab for Datalogi (Danish Association for Computer Science), Dansk Selskab for Operationsanalyse (Danish Association for Operational Research), DIFDATA (a branch of the Danish Association for Engineers especially interested in Computing), Dansk Selskab for Medicinsk Informatik (Danish Association of Medical Informatics) and Datalaererforeningens Folkeskolefraktion (a section of the Primary School Computing Teachers. Of these, Dansk Dataforening and DIFDATA account for about 90 % of the members of DANFIP. Dansk Dataforening's members are mainly managers and consultants. Members of DIFDATA are primarily engineers.

The role of these many professional organizations is to organize seminars, conferences, and participate in governmental bodies regulating areas of interest to present and future IT-professionals.

5.4 Involvement of IT professionals in new systems of professional relations

For several years IT professionals in Denmark have engaged in close cooperation with unions and user representatives in participatory design methods. Today this is the most common method of designing IT-systems, which is recommended also by the official Department of Administration.

Quality circles have been tried out in Denmark, but abandoned again. They seem to conflict with the ordinary consultative structures between management and employees. However, quality is receiving a lot of attention. Many companies have appointed a quality officer and have introduced new procedures.

5.5 Regulations or agreements in the field of professional ethics

Certain aspects of professional ethics are embedded in the two Co-operation Agreements (for the public and private labour markets respectively) and in the Public and Private Data Files Acts. However, in 1979, EDB-Rådet formulated a code of professional ethics which bears many similarities to the Ethical Code of the British Computer Society, which served as a starting point for discussions in Denmark. The code of professional ethics contains five guidelines on professional competence, consideration for user requirements, openness and impartiality, common honesty, and specialist obligations and specialist protection. However, it is a general impression that these guidelines are not very well known among IT-professionals.

FEDERAL REPUBLIC OF GERMANY

Jürgen REESE
Department of Economics
University of Kassel

1. Definition of "information technology professionals"

Information technology (IT) professionals are divided into nine main groups by the Federal Labour Office (Bundesanstalt für Arbeit):

- IT professionals - specialization not indicated (Datenverarbeitungsfachleute ohne nähere Angabe);
- system analysts, organizers (Systemanalytiker, Organisatoren);
- applications programmers (Anwendungsprogrammierer);
- system programmers (Systemprogrammierer);
- computer centre specialists (Rechenzentrumsfachleute);
- distribution specialists (Vertriebsfachleute, EDV);
- data processing dealers (Datenverarbeitungskaufleute);
- computer scientists (Informatiker, EDV);
- data processing coordinators (andere Datenverarbeitungskaufleute).

In a more detailed classification, the "Bundesanstalt für Arbeit" distinguishes almost 100 different occupations in the data-processing sector.

2. Labour market

2.1. Output of the Education System

Today there are about 150 000 IT professionals in the Federal Republic of Germany. Their educational background is shown in the following figures:

- 25 % possess a master's degree or equivalent;
- 63 % have had vocational training of between two or three years;
- 10 % have had no particular vocational training;
- 2 % have had some other relevant education or training.

The trend definitely favours higher qualifications.

The training of computer scientists at colleges and universities began on a significant scale in the Seventies. Thus, in the late Fifties and the Sixties, data processing was introduced and carried out by personnel without particular training and qualifications, by people who changed their jobs and by self-taught experts (1). Retraining and advanced training was mainly organized by the computer industry.

In recent years, the role of computer-sciences at universities and colleges has dramatically increased. The number of students in computer-science classes rose from 5 948 in 1975 (14 % female) to 29 675 in 1984 (16 % female). The number of graduates grew from 524 in 1977 to 2 700 in 1986 (estimation).

In spite of these high rates of growth, the output of the educational system does not match demand. There is a high and unsatisfied demand for computer scientists on the labour market which is estimated at 30 000 to 40 000 specialists.

---

(1) Dostal W., <u>Mit Schirm, Chip und Konsole</u>, Materialen zur Arbeitsmarkt- und Berufsforschung, Juni 1987, p 8.

2.2. Employment and Unemployment of IT Professionals

The fact that the educational system cannot produce a sufficient number of professionals suggests that the labour-market situation is between good and excellent for this professional group. This assessment can be illustrated by statistics of the institute for research on the labour market and professions of the Bundesanstalt für Arbeit (Federal Office for Labour).

Since 1978, the total number of IT professionals has increased by 50 % to 150 000 at present. The ratio of females is still low (16.5 %) but has increased slightly in recent years. This ratio is expected to continue to rise. In view of the shortage of staff, managers are obviously also ready to hire females.

In 1986, there were 5 248 registered unemployed IT professionals. This represents an unemployment ratio of 3.5 %. There is one vacancy for every two unemployed IT professionals. The following proportion of managers are looking for the specialists indicated (2):

- system analysts   48 %
- system programmers   30 %
- applications programmers   30 %
- data processing coordinators   20 %
- other   14 %

The significant increase in employment is accompanied by continuing unemployment and an increasing number of available jobs for IT professionals. This is firm evidence of the extraordinarily favourable labour-market situation facing IT professionals. However, the difference in qualifications has to be considered. At and above college-degree level, the number of available jobs exceeds the number of registered unemployed, with five vacancies for every unemployed IT professional.

---

(2) Sandschepper G., Herr der Rechner: ein schwer regierbares Reich, in Online, n 6/1988, p 61

The chances of getting a job are estimated to be good in future. The following reasons are mentioned in the literature (3):

- The full extent of computer capacity has not yet been attained, though it must be met very soon.

- Office automation is still far below potential.

- The increasing complexity of the systems calls for highly qualified service and maintenance personnel.

- Data protection problems have not yet been effectivly solved.

- Data processing will be a basic element of the future communication society.

At the same time, certain factors indicate a decrease in demand for IT professionals:

- Software production will be constantly formalized and rationalized, with the result that productivity will increase.

- Programming languages will become easier to use and accelerate programme production.

- The increased use of standard software means a saving of programming capacities.

- At some time in the future all standard and special programmes will be written.

---

(3) Dostal W., op. cit.

Considering different arguments, W. DOSTAL, who is one of the most respected experts in this sector, comes to the following conclusion:

" In other sectors, engineers are in great demand, though new and innovative technologies are still rarely applied. This experience suggests that the demand for IT professionals is more likely to increase than decrease. In particular, the transition from the production of new programmes to the servicing, modification and adaptation of existing programmes will strengthen the demand for EDP-personnel in the longer term. A decrease in the demand for IT professionals seems improbable." (4)

2.3. Labour market regulation processes

As expected, the increase in the number of IT professionals is not constant over several years. The lower rates of increase at the beginning of the Eighties were obviously due to the economic recession in the Federal Republic of Germany.

The decreasing demand for hardware and software as well as the keen competition on the EDP-market is forcing producers and distributors to make qualitative and quantitative improvements in their selling activities. As a consequence, these firms are in search of more professionals who can be assigned to marketing and distribution.

The consulting firm Scientific Control Systems (SCS) thinks that this trend is again developing in Germany at present. Its analysis of requirements came to the conclusion that, already in 1987, 16 % of all demand can be attributed to these branches. For purpose of comparison, the figure was less than 10 % in 1986 (5).

---

(4) Dostal W., op. cit. p 7.

(5) Streicher H., Karrierechancen für den DV-Profil, Online, n[2/1988, p 80

Another regulatory factor for the employment of IT professionals are the so-called "head hunters". Their intimate market knowledge enables them to make direct contact with candidates for high-level management positions. This tendency was confirmed by the above-mentioned SCS analysis. It seems that the number of vacancies advertised in newspapers will be reduced as a consequence of this development. It is reported that more and more enterprises prefer to engage head hunters, even for high-qualified specialists.

All this information provides considerable evidence that IT professionals enjoy a favourable situation on the labour market. Their average annual income confirms this assessment.

The highest wages are paid in consulting firms, the lowest in the public services. The annual income of IT professionals was between DM 60 000 and DM 100 000 in 1984.

There are many factors determining the annual income of IT professionals, the most important being:

- professional experience;

- managerial position: the bonus increases with the number of a personnel for whom one is responsible;

- degrees: people with a doctorate receive an annual supplement of between DM 20 000 and DM 25 000 compared with people holding only diplomas; there is no or little difference between the income of university and college graduates;

- the range of activities: income increases when organizational activities are incorporated into the job description;

- sex: women earn DM 16 000 less on average; this difference cannot be explained by the lower average age of the women employed;

- geographical location: in contrast to wages in other sectors, there is no difference between the north and the south of the country for EDP-professionals. However, city size and the type of region (rural or industrial) do make a difference.

3. Social aspects and trends

3.1. Skills and work organization

As regards factors other than wages, the working conditions and vocational situation of IT professionals do not appear to be as favourable. One of these factors is the working week. With the exception of the computer industry, long working weeks are not unusual. Only one quarter of IT professionals work 40 hours per week on average. Three-quarters work longer, as the following breakdown shows:

- 28 % between 41 and 45 hours;
- 24 % between 46 and 50 hours;
- 17 % over 50 hours.

The differences between the sectors may be of interest. In research, education and training 27 % work over 50 hours, in the computer industry 11 %, among users 9 % and in other sectors (particularly consultants) 26 %. These differences are explained by TRAUTWEIN-KALMS as follows:

"One should assume that the differences cannot be attributed solely to positions of leadership (individual work contracts) but possibly also to the personality structure and intrinsic motivation of the employed. The differences may also be largely explained by the lack of protection in the status of employees, the organization of interests at firm level and the level of unionization. Particularly in poorly organized software houses (development, programming, consulting etc.), work conditions are influenced by full schedules, fear of the loss of employment (contracts on projects), competition and concern about mistakes. In this hotbed, atmospheres readiness to work overtime, to work more and to work more intensively increases." (6)

---

(6) Trautwein-Kalms G., <u>Arbeitsbedingungen qualifizierter Angestellter</u>, Arbeitspapier 22 der Projektgruppe, Humanisierung der Arbeit, Düsseldorf 1988, p 27.

A convention organized by the HBV (Trading & Retail, Banking and Insurances) labour union, which has shop stewards in the software industry, came to the conclusion that "overtime working is widespread. Often, it is not even recorded and certainly not sufficiently remunerated or compensated by free hours. In addition, even vacation time is not used because of indispensable work." Trautwein-Kalms states that, in some cases, employees in the software sector work up to 500 hours overtime per year without any additional payment.

3.2. Contracts, careers and professional mobility

There are no statistics concerning the drafting of work contracts in the Federal Republic of Germany. However, there is some evidence that many enterprises favour limited work contracts. There are also few or incomplete data relating to the career of IT professionals. Statistics are often collated by large private training organizations. They reveal only the careers of participants in their courses. The statistics are also used for marketing purposes with the aim of demonstrating the quality of the training offered. For instance, the Computer Bildungs Institut (CBI) in Wiesbaden announced that only 35 % of trained organization programmers are still in their first job after three years. In 1984, the percentage was still 65 %. In 1987, 6 % of all participants had reached the position of data processing co-ordinator compared with 1 % in 1984. These figures suggest that the lack of IT professionals produces good career opportunities.

A more detailed career study was carried out by the consulting firm SCS and the journal "Online". This study relates only to the most senior levels. As a relevant conclusion, the study notes that professional standards rose during recent years. Today, there is a particular demand for management and leadership abilities as well as for business qualifications. This trend can be inferred from the fact that the proportion of senior EDP managers who have no university degree has continually decreased. The growing importance of training in business administration also provides some evidence for this hypothesis.

Most of the EDP-professionals in leading positions come from similar branches in other enterprises. It may also be of interest that the importance of hardware producers and the universities as a reserve has diminished. The EDP-service centres (software houses, consulting firms, service centres) are becoming increasingly important, however. This can be taken as an indicator that, apart from technical knowledge, many more qualifications are now demanded.

3.3. Training and retraining requirements

The high intensity of the work done by IT professionals restricts their opportunities for advanced training and the acquisition of qualifications. The Gesellschaft für Informatik (the German association of computer scientists) carried out a survey which indicates a high but unsatisfied interest in qualifications. The time spent on personnel qualifications and advanced training is by far the highest in the research and educational sector, amounting to 33.8 hours per month on average. Employees in the computer industry spend 21.5 hours per month, on such activities. Much of the training spills over into leisure time.

Only one third of IT professionals are content with the training and retraining programmes offered . The best estimates can be found in the research, education and training sector. Lack of time is cited as the main reason for discontent in all sectors. This reflects the high intensity of the work, although the unwillingness of employers to support the advanced training of employees financially is a relevant factor. This is all the more remarkable in that total expenditure on the advanced training of IT professionals amounts to some DM 1 800 million per year. One third of this amount is supplied by the Bundesanstalt für Arbeit, the rest being provided by the private economy.

3.4. Increasing or decreasing professionalism

Many indicators suggest an increasing specialization of IT professionals in the Federal Republic of Germany. First, there is the above-mentioned shock of vocational titles in advertisements. Almost every professional activity acquires known professional titles. The fast change of titles is particularly problematic. Since technological development is surging ahead, the statistical categories have to be constantly updated.

However, it is also the sheer multiplicity of different computer systems which promotes specialization. This becomes obvious when wanted ads are considered. In many cases, they call for existing knowledge about specific products, 5 671 of which were analyzed in an inquiry conducted by the Data Control Institute in Munich.

The specialization trend is confirmed by the SCS personnel consulting firm in its analysis of vacancies (7). This study correlates also the specialization and the training level: the more specialized the offered job, the less important is the university degree which is otherwise a necessary precondition.

Another indicator of increasing specialization is the availability of particular training programmes which prepare professionals for specific sectors. The programme for computer specialists in the construction sector offered by the Technische Hochschule, Berlin (University) in conjunction with the computer firm Norsk Data is an example. This programme is particularly suitable for engineers, technicians and businessmen who want to study the use of computers apart from their regular job. The course is not primarily directed to IT professionals but offers the opportunity for employment in computing on completion.

4. Government policies

The Federal and State Governments are making great efforts to meet the demand for IT professionals. The planning committee for the construction of universities established a working group to analyze demand in the States in 1985. The group was to report on the status of computer-science in universities and colleges and present specific proposals. The group also considered appropriate means of adapting computer-science equipment to the latest developments (8).

In its report, the working group states that the personnel and technical situation at universities and colleges is far from adequate to satisfy demand. The States now intend to improve the position of computer-science in different ways. It must, however, be pointed out that some of these provisions are still being discussed internally. Others are already agreed. Thus, the following information is only provisionally comparable.

---

(7) Streicher H., op. cit. p 80.

(8) Bassler R., Informatiker im Beruf, in Beitrage zur Arbeitsmarkt und Berufsforschung, vol 106, Nürnberg, 1987.

The States intend to increase the number of university places for students from 2 598 to 4 046. To cope with this growth, a total of 132 additional jobs will be created. The proposed investment in the technological infrastructure of computer-science totals DM 63.7 million. The activities of the States of Baden-Württemberg, Hamburg, Hesse and North-Rhine-Westphalia deserve particular mention in this context.

Regarding the colleges, the States intend to increase the number of places for new students from 2 727 to 3 798. Even so, capacity in the personnel sector will be increased by only 55 posts to cope with this expansion. The planned investment of DM 0.8 million is very small compared with the plans for the universities.

The above-mentioned working group recommends a particular programme for the improvement of computer-science equipment. The State and Federal Governments have earmarked some DM 40 million for the computer-science programme. In a second stage, the amount available will rise to DM 100 million.

At the sectoral and local level there are many specific public programmes for the training and retraining of IT professionals. Most of these are organized as pilot projects to test specific forms of training.

In general, the promotion of vocational training enjoys high importance as a means of meeting the demand for IT professionals in the Federal Republic of Germany. The number of participants in all classes, courses, studies and the like concerned with advanced vocational training, retraining and on-the-job training has dramatically increased in recent years. Whereas only 2 500 employees participated in training programmes for IT professionals in 1980, over 20 000 did so in 1986. The proportion of women increased continually over the same period.

5. Professional associations and industrial relations

5.1. Role of professional groups and associations

The "Gesellschaft für Informatik" plays the most important role among all professional groups and associations. Since its introduction, the study of computer-science ("Informatik") at colleges and universities has been strongly influenced by it. The association did not merely concern itself with technological developments but also considered social and societal consequences. Just recently, the association has been asked by the Federal Minister for Research and Technology to comment on preliminary draft legislation of the Federal Government, which outlines strategies for the development of computer-science as an academic subject and information technology in general.

The association also maintains contact with the Federal Ministry of Economic Affairs. This cooperation covers computer-science as a key technology for a compatible economy, problems of computer crime, advanced training and the labour market.

The "Gesellschaft für Mathematik und Datenverarbeitung" (GMD) is also very important. The activities of this large research organization are focused on the further development of information technology and its application. Apart from these two large organizations there are some other institutions which deal with specific questions and tasks in the field of information technology. For instance, scientists and IT professionals founded the "Deutsche Gesellschaft für Informationstechnik und Recht" (German Society for Information Technology and Law) in 1986. This organization encourages and supports the analysis and solution of problems which are thrown up by information technology. It also promotes the application of information technology in the legal sector and the development of a legal framework for the use of information technology in general.

5.2. Unionization, collective agreements

In general IT professionals are not organized in unions in the Federal Republic of Germany. However, the unions are attempting to change this situation, essentially concentrating their atack on the poor working conditions in the consulting sector and smaller software houses.

There are almost no wage contracts or contracts at company level which guarantee wages and regulate the wage structure. This is particularly true of the computer industry. In addition, the wages of IT professionals exceed the levels of the negotiated wage structure. This may be a reason for employee attitudes towards unions.

5.3. Professional ethics

Ethics in computer-science are relatively important in the Federal Republic of Germany. The above-mentioned Gesellschaft für Informatik (GI) has already done pioneer work in earlier reports. Questions regarding the societal and social responsibility of computer scientists are dealt with by a special section of the association: the Section 8 "Informatics and Society". More recently, Section 8 publicly opposed the introduction of identity cards which can be read by machines.

Another indicator of the high value of ethics for computer scientists is the foundation of the FIFF (Forum Informatiker für Frieden und gesellschaftliche Verantwortung, Forum of Informaticians for Peace and Social Responsibility). This organization was founded by over 200 people at the University of Bonn in 1984. It was prompted by increasing fears of the social impact of computers on working conditions, the military sector and private and public life. The statutes of the association cite the following aims:

- demonstration of the importance of information technology and of the work of IT professionals for military purposes;
- examination of the military influences on the development of information technology;
- identification of unreliability in complex information systems;
- provision of information for professional colleagues, political decision-makers and the public; initiation of discussions to encourage the responsibility;
- demonstration of the relevance of information technology and of the work of IT professionals for rationalization and control functions;
- combination of the responsibility for the societal impact of information technology with responsibility for research and development in this field.

Today FIFF has about 750 members in almost all fields of computer-science: research and training, computer industry, applications, journalism, large enterprises and smaller software houses. Since 1984 the membership has increased almost fourfold.

GREECE

Marcos NIKOLINAKOS
Institute for the Study of the Greek Economy
Athens

Specific studies of the labour market for information technology (IT) professionals have not been conducted by any of the institutions involved in this area. Most of the literature centres on the impact of information technology on employment in general, rather than on employment conditions and the demand for IT professionals.

Data were collected by the Greek Productivity Center in two surveys carried out in 1975 and 1980. Conditions have changed drastically since then. The third such survey is being carried out this year, and the initial findings will be released early next year.

Another survey has been planned and will be carried out in 1989 by the Directorate for the Development of Informatics. This survey, which will cover the public sector, is expected to reveal aspects of the information technology profession which have not been the object of a formal study to date.

The third source of information is Strategic International, a private consulting firm. The advantage of the surveys conducted by this firm is their annual updates. Their shortcoming is their failure to disclose the methodology used. These surveys cover the whole informatics spectrum, i.e. hardware, software, production, imports, etc.

1. Definition of "information technology professionals"

For all practical purposes, "information technology professionals" are considered to be those who had a formal education in information technology. Even lower-level personnel in information technology professions have received some education and training within the formal educational system or outside it. In Greece, it is not only the formal educational system that produces professionals; a number of free-studies workshops produce lower level professionals. No professionals are produced by vocational high schools in the State system.

2. Labour market

Until recently, all professionals with university degrees received their education abroad, primarily in the United Kingdom and secondarily in the United States, West Germany and other European countries. In the 80's, university-level education in information technology started slowly but steadily. Today there are independent departments in three universities and three technical colleges. The annual output of graduate students rose from 45 in 1982 to 919 in 1985 and 1 532 in 1988. Of the students in 1988, 54 % graduated in hardware engineering, 10 % in business informatics and 36 % in systems design and programming (software).

As the number of degree-holders from local Universities increases the labour market will eventually be restructured and some friction between foreign and national degree-holders can be expected.

Besides formal education, there are a number of free-studies workshops producing programmers and operators. There are eleven such workshops with a total student body of approximately four thousand high-school graduates.

The discussion of employment and unemployment does not centre on IT professionals, but on the impact of the introduction of new information technology on employment in general.

In a questionnaire addressed to companies concerning the relative difficulty or ease they faced in filling vacant IT posts, companies replied that it was most difficult to fill systems-analyst positions and relatively easy to engage operators.

Empirical evidence shows that the market for all kinds of IT professionals is still affected by shortages. One source of such information is the wanted ads in the daily press. Wages are comparatively higher that those of other professions. In the public sector, certain allowances are granted to IT professionals.

3. Social aspects and trends

Specific studies of the subject have not been conducted. Much will be revealed in the study which is to be carried out shortly by the Greek Productivity Centre. The study is much broader in scope and is expected to provide data on social aspects and trends as a by-product.

The following statistical data which were compiled in the 1980 study may be of some relevance to this section of the report. In 1980, the distribution of IT professionals by job category appears to have been as follows:

- EDP managers 10.2 %
- System engineers 2.9 %
- System analysts 8.3 %
- Analyst-programmers 16.6 %
- Programmers 15.3 %
- Programmer-operators 5.0%
- Operators 21.6 %
- Input/output control 20.1 %

This survey revealed a total of 2 162 IT professionals, excluding the 1 843 data-entry operators. A breakdown by category and sex shows that women account for 87.2 % of the data-entry operators and 56.5 % of the I/O controllers, but only 6.5 % of the system engineers, 11 % of the system analysts and 19.4 % of the analyst-programmers.

Another interesting piece of information concerns the educational background of males and females. This distribution confirms that information, since job levels correlate directly with educational levels. A number of papers have been published on the subject of the status of women in the IT professions, and these are included in the bibliography. All of them are opinion articles rather than research articles.

Since 1980, the number of degree-holders has increased substantially and in the coming years technical college graduates will become more important; this may cause some friction between the latter group and university graduates.

An article on "The Strategic Development of Informatics in Public Administration" provides some statistical data on the distribution of IT professionals by job classification in the public sector:

Managers	5.1 %
Analyst-programmers	21.4 %
Operators	7.7 %
Data-entry operators	36.6 %
Other	29.2 %

4. Government Policies

Government strategic policies are decided by the Government Council on Informatics. Strategic plans are drawn up by the Technical Council on Informatics. The implementation of government policies is overseen by the Directorate for the Development of Informatics which is a staff directorate of the Ministry of the Presidency.

The Government is highly instrumental in the diffusion of IT in many ways. It helps local administration units as well as government agencies, offices and services to introduce information technology.

In the National School of Public Administration, information technology courses are taught to initiate the new generation of public servants in this area.

5. Professional associations and industrial relations

There are four professional organizations for IT professionals: the Hellenic Computer Scientists Association, the Hellenic Informatics Institute, the Hellenic Informatics Association, and the Computer-Personnel Association.

The first is a scientific and scholarly association, membership of which is restricted to university graduates. It has been very active in organizing meetings and other activities of professional interest. The Hellenic Informatics Institute is a branch of the Hellenic Management Association. Its members are managers. The third association is more of a professional than a scientific body. It has 280 members and is open to university graduates with at least four years' experience. The aim of the association is to promote information technology in Greece. The fourth is a trade union with members drawn from the public sector. It has not succeeded in promoting professional interests in that sector.

Owing to the comparatively higher salaries of IT professionals, trade unionism has not had a significant impact in this area.

SPAIN

Juan Ignacio PALACIO [1]

Universitad Complutense, Madrid

1. Definition of IT professionals

In countries like Spain, the relatively poor diffusion of information technologies and the lack of connection between the limited R&D activity and practical applications make for additional difficulties and ambiguity in the definition of Information Technology (IT) professionals.

On the one hand, the educational system still lacks training programmes which are specifically designed to qualify part of the labour force for employment in professions related to these technologies and, on the other, the professional qualifications that we are interested in are not sufficiently established in the employee categories used by companies. At all events, we rely on a double criterion covering both the jobs done (activity profile) and the type of know-how concerned (know-how or educational profile).

On that basis, IT professionals are defined as those engaged in such jobs or activities as research and development, design and projects, production, operation and maintenance, sales and marketing, management and administration, top management and training, in the fields of electronics, computer science, telecommunications and industrial production and who are qualified in such disciplines as electronics technology, electronics circuits and equipment, software technology, computer architecture and technology, telematics engineering, radiocommunications, systems and process control.

---

[1]   Co-authors are: Mikel BUSEA, José MOLERO.

These types of qualification or required knowledge correspond to the following formal qualifications or specialities in the Spanish educational system:

a) Higher Degrees (five years): Graduates in Physics, Computer Science, Mathematics, Aeronautical Engineering, Industrial Engineering and Telecommunications Engineering;

b) Intermediate Degrees (three years): Diplomas in Computer Science, Technical Aeronautical Engineering and Technical Telecommunications Engineering.

This definition excludes pure information technology users and those who fail to attain a minimum level of formal education and professional qualifications.

2. Labour market

2.1. Output of the education system

The ambiguity in the definition of professions creates a glaring deficiency in the statistics showing the output of the educational system: as there is no direct link between certain types of formal education and the training of IT professionals, the use of educational statistics is inadequate for our purposes. All of this means that it is very difficult to determine educational output, and impossible in the case of vocational training. Fortunately, we do not have the same problem with regard to University Education, since FUNDESCO research (2) has provided reliable estimates for the 1982-1985 period and forecasts for 1986-1988. Henceforth, therefore, we will refer exclusively to university education.

This FUNDESCO research estimates that in 1988 the output of university degrees in IT-related disciplines will approach 4 500. Since 1982, the annual output has risen by 220 %. In 1988, nearly 2 500 higher degrees were awarded, although the figure for intermediate degrees was below 2 000.

---

(2) FUNDESCO, Formación de técnicos e investigadores en tecnologías de la información, Madrid, 1986.

This research reveals several points of interest:

- Firstly, there has been a substantial increase in the number of university graduates whose studies qualify them for employment in IT-related professions. Thus, between 1982 and 1985 there was a 49.5 % increase, and forecasts for 1988 suggest that the annual-output figures for the first year considered will be multiplied by 2.2. These increases are undoubtedly due to the faster diffusion of information technologies. This means that the greater demand for qualified staff in this area is putting great pressure on the educational system, and requiring it to provide the right training.

- Secondly, it must be pointed out that university training in the field of information technologies takes place in a wide variety of centres where this type of programme has been introduced. That is why the Faculties of Computer Science and the Technical Schools for Telecommunications Engineering are the only centres where the academic approach is exclusively focussed on information technologies. In the other cases considered, the courses involve other specialities that are not related to the field under examination here. This shows that the educational system cannot yet completely meet the emerging requirements of information technologies. As will be seen later on, this situation accounts for a certain variation in degrees, so that jobs offered on the market may be filled by people with degrees in different disciplines.

- Lastly, we should mention that the number of people holding higher degrees is 30 % above that for intermediate degree-holders, which reflects the fact that university students generally prefer longer courses. In this connection, of the total number of university students, there are 2.7 times more students registered for higher degrees than for intermediate degrees. This means that the disproportion between university students doing higher and intermediate degrees in the IT field is smaller than for university students as a whole.

2.2. Employment of IT professionals

The difficulties noted with regard to educational-output data are even greater in the case of employment and unemployment, where there is an even more serious lack of data. In fact, neither the Survey on the Working Population, drawn up by the National Institute of Statistics, nor the data provided by the National Institute of Employment give us any help in identifying the group of workers covered by this report. Thus, on the basis of official figures, it is impossible to know how many people are employed in the IT field and how they are divided into professional categories. Moreover, it is impossible to discover what the unemployment figures for this group of workers are.

Different sources relating to in the electronics industry and computer and telecommunications services indicate that the electronics industry witnessed a 6.7 % decrease in employment between 1982 and 1986, whilst employment increased by 26.4 % in the computer-services sector and 2.3 % in that of telecommunications services.

On the whole, therefore, employment in sectors producing IT-related hardware and services has remained stable and there is no indication that it will increase in future. The material conditions in which the diffusion of information technology takes place do not favour increasing employment in the industries and service sectors which produce it. Moreover, future expansion could quite easily be based on increased productivity in these industries and service sectors through the use of the technologies that they themselves generate.

2.3. Labour supply and demand

This conclusion is in marked contrast to the results of other studies which have forecast a spectacular increase in the demand for graduates with higher and intermediate degrees in IT-related subjects. The most well-known study (3) estimated that there would be a need for 21 250 more such professionals between 1985 and 1988. Of these, 11 260 would be employed in the field of computer services, 2 720 in telecommunications and the remaining 6 910 in the electronics industry.

---

(3) Castells M. & al., <u>Nuevas tecnologías, economía y sociedad en España</u>, Ed. Alianza, Madrid, 1986, pp. 923 onwrds

These figures would seem to be excessively high if we consider that, during the first two years of this period (1985 and 1986), employment in the computer-services sector went up by 510, in the telecommunications sector by 252 and in the electronics industry by 1 181. These data take account of the net creation of employment in all types of jobs and do not apply solely to graduates with higher degrees, making the overestimation of demand in the abovementioned study extremely high.

Moreover, the FUNDESCO study, which was mentioned in the previous section and based on the demand estimated by CASTELLS et al. and which contrasted its data on the output of graduates holding higher and intermediate degrees with this estimate, forecast a deficit of 12 820 such professionals between 1985 and 1988. The breakdown of this deficit according to professional qualifications and economic sectors shows that software technology and telematics engineering are the main areas of mismatch between supply and demand (accounting, respectively, for 45 % and 38 % of the total deficit). Once again it is useful to compare these data with available data on changing patterns of employment in the electronics industry and computer and telecommunication services; these show that FUNDESCO's estimates are much higher than the actual demand for graduates.

Something similar is revealed by more moderate estimates, such as that produced by the consultants NTP for the Official College of Telecommunications Engineers and the Spanish Association of Telecommunications Engineers (4). In this study, which was based on a survey of 50 electronics, computer and communications companies, the demand for higher-level graduates was put at 1 287 for the period 1985-1990.

If these forecasts overestimate the capacity of the electronics industry and the computer and telecommunications sectors to absorb the output of the educational system, one might expect unemployment among IT graduates with higher and intermediate degrees as a result of the increased output.

Although there are no data to corroborate this hypothesis, it does not, in fact, seem to be correct. Information obtained from different experts shows that there is no unemployment among IT-professionals. This means that, although the sectors which are directly involved in the production of goods and services that incorporate information technologies have a limited capacity for generating employment, there are other areas of economic activity in which IT professionals are required.

---

(4) Meza R., Garcia I., Perez J., <u>Demanda de ingenieros de telecomunicación para el quinquenio 1985-1990</u>, cit. in FUNDESCO (1986), op. cit., pp. 140-153.

A recent study (EIDE project) suggested that companies prefer higher degrees in telecommunications engineering, with special emphasis on systems control, and physicists who are specialized in automatic computation to people with more specific qualifications in computer science. Although consultancy and engineering firms play an important role in the introduction and diffusion of information technologies, very few are involved in the most complex areas and the number of IT-professionals employed in the sector is also very small.

3. Social aspects and trends

3.1. Job profiles

The majority of IT professionals in Spain are engaged in the development of software applications and design and projects for installing computer systems to the neglect of basic R&D and administrative and management activities, which means that hardware and primary innovation are relatively underdeveloped. This unfavourable state of affairs is offset by the import of basic technologies from abroad, which accounts for the vast amount of technical/commercial activities in this sector and the relatively low level of qualifications and experience required.

The principal growth in demand for information-technology professionals is in those service in which the main requirement is for design and projects activities. This increase is much smaller in industry, where there is greater emphasis on R&D and sales and applications. National firms carry out more R&D and design and project activities, and require less experience than multinational companies which give priority to commercial tasks and to operation and maintenance and require a larger proportion of graduates with previous experience.

3.2. Careers and mobility

The lack of machinery for institutionalizing and giving social recognition to new IT qualifications is clearly shown by the absence of any official work contracts for professionals doing these jobs.

Generally speaking, skills are acquired on the job. A large number of IT professionals have no clearly defined qualifications or professional training. Companies do not turn to the outside market in order to meet new requirements for technical staff or professionals but tend to make changes in their organizational structure, thereby increasing job mobility. In addition to these requirements, there is a demand for super-specialists; although the need is very limited in terms of numbers, these people occupy key posts in the organizational structure of the firm. This last group is characterized by the greatest external mobility and the highest salaries.

3.3. Training and retraining requirements

As a result of the situation outlined above, training requirements are not mainly vocational or occupational, but relate to the basic content of the professions concerned.

The problem lies in the fact that this gives rise to a sort of "vicious circle". The absence of information technology professionals leads to improvised "adaptation" training on the job, which is sometimes not even perceived as a lack of training, but as a gradual, inevitable process of change. The result is that we get "devalued" information technology professionals who cannot, strictly, be considered as such. This lack of professionalism reinforces a production structure which has little capacity for assimilating technology and in which the use of new information technologies has priority over research and technological innovation. Thus, as a recent study pointed out, the short supply of these professionals imposes restrictions on the demand for their services: "The shortage of information technology professionals limits the demand for such staff in the medium term. What is more, this limits the user's training requirements, since it works as a deterrent against introducing technology itself; or else it impoverishes and impedes technological implementation" (5).

The need for training and retraining is essentially located somewhere between true information technology professionals and the "users" of these technologies. Here there are a variety of training and retraining requirements, depending on the different production areas and the previous training of workers affeced by technological change.

---

(5) Villarejo E., <u>Necesidades de formación inducidas por las tecnologías de concepción y diseño asistido por ordenador y software integrado de gestión</u>, FUNDESCO, Madrid, 1988, p. 42

An ascending scale of training requirements could be drawn up. As a result of the situation described, explicit training requirements are often very low. Employees need no more than all-round knowledge, and a capacity for teaching themselves and adapting to change ("polyvalent" and "mobile"). It is a question of adapting easily and quickly to changing responsibilities in a situation in which professionalism is not very highly valued (6).

Although more stringent training requirements are clearly necessary, the corresponding abilities may sometimes be more latent or potential. The need to get up-to-date or to perfect skills often calls for a specific training process, which could be of any length, from 40 hours to two academic years or more (7). In many cases, the greatest difficulty arises from the fact that requirements do not fit the traditional patterns of professional or occupational training. Compared with conventional approaches to professional training and retraining, based on learning operative methods and manual or similar skills and passive integration into a given organizational structure, a greater capacity for abstraction and the acquisition of theoretical knowledge is required, together with a capacity for initiative, responsibility and creativity within an organizational environment which is constantly changing. Thus, a more comprehensive type of training becomes the norm - one which not only imparts basic specialized knowledge but which also increases the recipients' capacity for abstraction and theoretical reasoning, affects personal motivation and promotes active employee participation.

---

(6) Homs O., Kruse W., Ordovas R., Pries L., Cambios de cualificación en las empresas españolas, Fundación IESA, Madrid, 1987.

(7) Segovia R., Zaccagnini J.L., Nuevas tecnologías y formación ocupacional en España, FUNDESCO, Madrid, 1988

4. Government policy

The deficiencies of the Spanish educational system are particularly strongly felt in the case of IT-professionals. There is a great imbalance between intermediate-level and higher graduates, and between technical-scientific and humanities courses. There are more higher- than intermediate-level graduates, and more humanities courses than technical-scientific courses. The diversity of types of degree is very slight, and the existence of "closed" study plans does not allow students to move from one centre to another to complete their training. Lastly, postgraduate training is practically non-existent, which, to a large extent, reflects not only the small amount of research done, but also the absence of links between research work, which is almost totally monopolized by University and State institutes and the world of production and business. The process of university reform, which is now under way, is intended to remove some of these deficiencies. There is an increase in the variety of degrees, especially short-cycle degrees, and less rigid curricula. The idea is to create new degrees in the IT field. A greater number would be three-year courses with the possibility of extending the cycle (two years more), with no extra training.

In addition, there is also what is known as "occupational training". This is directly linked to professional training or retraining requirements. It is coordinated by the National Institute of Employment (INEM), which comes under the Ministry of Labour, and is given at this Institute's training centres or at centres which collaborate with different public or private bodies. In the latter case, there is collaboration with employer's organizations and Unions, as well as with private enterprise.

It is more difficult to assess occupational training as a whole. Generally speaking, despite the fact that it is theoretically directly linked to the needs of training and retraining the workforce, there is very little correlation between the courses offered and the requirements of the production system or the demand for initial qualifications from those who may possibly benefit from them. Moreover, it is basically directed at the unemployed, thus ignoring the retraining needs of people already in employment (8).

Public institutions like the INEM (National Institute of Employment) and the COIES (Student Orientation and Information Centres) play a very limited role as intermediaries on the IT professionals labour market.

---

(8) Megia E., Vilarejo E., El papel de los interlocutores sociales en la formación profesional en España, Study carried out for CEDEFOP (Berlin), Madrid, 1988

5. Professional associations and industrial relations

There is only one specific association of IT professionals, the Official College of Telecommunications Engineers. The other associations are really enterprise associations with commercial objectives, although they incorporate certain professional rules in their Statutes.

There is no specific union nor any specific section within Spanish unions for these workers. They are generally included in their respective sectors, together with other workers. This means that there are no collective agreements specifically applicable to these professionals. There are, however, specific sections or clauses in the different company, branch or sectoral agreements which cover a significant number of such professionals.

FRANCE

Abdélaziz EL FAKIR, Nicole AZOULAY
Economics Department (CERCA)
Paris University VIII

1. DEFINING "COMPUTER PROFESSIONALS"

In accordance with the CEREQ study on "computer-related jobs"(1), it has been decided to distinguish four main <u>employment categories</u> for the purposes of this study:

a) The SYSTEMS category covers the functions performed by the designers of the new hardware and basic software, and the tasks involved in optimising the performance of existing systems.

b) The APPLICATIONS category covers software activities relating to applications developed on the basis of standard software, or the development of specific software packages with the aid of programming languages, in the fields of scientific (computer centres, statistical estimates, research), industrial and business computing.

c) The OPERATING AND MAINTENANCE category covers all tasks linked to the various processing operations performed in computer centres in terms of the production and running of these centres, as well as the prevention of breakdowns and repairwork in computer installations.

d) The COMMERCIAL category constitutes a link between the user firm and the hardware or software supplier.

---

(1) CEREQ, <u>Computer-related professions,</u> (2 vol.), French Documentation, Paris, 1987.

2. JOB MARKET

2.1 Diplomas in Computing

Any attempt to deal with the subject of education and degrees in computing calls for a precise definition of the criteria involved. The fact is that many training courses adopt the computer studies "label", even in cases where computing accounts for only a few hours in the curriculum. In the studies quoted in this document a minimum requirement of 500 hours of computer studies per year was fixed. This 500-hour minimum either forms part of a course in which computing is the core subject or constitutes a computer studies option.

This report is exclusively concerned with higher education, i.e. only degree-level studies have been taken into account.

In France, higher education in computer studies takes place at three main levels:

- upper secondary school certificate + 2 years higher education for technicians
- upper secondary school certificate + 4/5 years higher education for engineers
- upper secondary school certificate + 7 or more years higher education for doctors of science

Graduates (9 000 in 1988) are evenly divided between those who follow up their education with 2 years of higher education and those who study for a further 4 or 5 years. Doctors of science account for only 4% of graduates.

a) BTS

The BTS, or Senior Technician Certificate, covers two subgroups: the first, entitled "Computer Services", was created in 1981 and renamed "Management Computing" in 1987. The second was created in 1982 and was entitled "Industrial Computer Studies". Fifty percent of students study for this diploma in state establishments while the other fifty percent study in private institutions; 94% of students in this subgroup already hold the upper secondary school certificate.

The "Management Computing" subgroup currently has 1 725 students. The new syllabus includes training in business studies, the technical environment and tuition in computer-related negotiations.

b) DUT

The DUT, or University Degree in Technology, was created in 1966 and provides a 2-year training course for high-calibre technicians.

In 1983, at the height of its success among employers, the number of applications for this sort of training reached impressive proportions, with 55 000 applications for fewer than 3 000 places. At present, the number of applicants is approximately 27 000, i.e. a fifty per cent drop. Nevertheless, even though the corresponding job prospects are less secure than a few years ago, the DUT remains a highly coveted qualification. Often firms are unable to find graduates who have spent 4 or 5 years in higher education and regard the DUT as a useful alternative.

The DUT diploma enables certain students to follow up their studies with a Master's Degree or entry to an engineering college. This route is proving increasingly popular with students who thus already hold a professional qualification that is highly valued on the job market.

c) Master's Degree

The master's degree in computing lasts for two years and follows on from the DEUG (first degree, 2 years post-secondary education). Firms are eager to recruit such degree-holders who have also obtained a DESS or DEA (see below), but the MIAGE is considered more desirable than a master's degree when the latter is not accompanied by other qualifications.

d) MIAGE

The MIAGE, or Master's Degree in Management-Related Computing, involves a 2-year course and follows on from the DEUG. It was created in 1971 and offers a highly distinctive combination of studies. The initial selection procedure is succeeded by an intensive course of studies (1 600 hours, spread over 2 years) and long periods of outside training. The status of the qualification is reviewed every four years.
Although not as highly qualified as students who have spent 5 years in post-secondary eduction, students who successfully complete the MIAGE course enjoy exactly the same career pattern as engineers, owing to the respect which their qualification commands among employees: 18 universities award this degree which is obtained by between 90 and 100% of the students enrolled.

e) The Magistère

The Magistère is a nationally accredited university degree, involving a 3-year course which follows on either from the DEUG or the DUT; it was instituted in 1985 and has much in common with the qualifications offered by the engineering colleges. This particular type of training has attracted company investment and their interest will rapidly become apparent when 1988 yields the first crop of graduates - all of whom will have spent 5 years in higher education.

f) Engineering colleges

Although many engineering colleges claim to offer computer training, only 15 award a diploma in computing while 21 offer an option involving at least 500 hours of tuition, covering three main areas: general, industrial and management computing.

g) DESS

The DESS, or Diploma in Specialized Higher Studies, is a post-graduate university diploma which lasts for one year. It is orientated towards professionalism and specialization. Applicants, who include students with Masters's degrees or the MIAGE (and sometimes even engineering-college graduates) are selected on the basis of their academic record and an interview.

The DESS is held in high regard by employers who recognize and appreciate the skills which these young graduates have to offer. Newly qualified specialists have no difficulty finding jobs: holders of the DESS qualification are employed as engineers, under the same conditions as engineers.

h) DEA

The DEA, or Diploma in Specialized Studies, involves a one-year course and follows 4 years' post-secondary education (master's degree) or graduation from engineering college. The diploma provides an opening into lecturing and research.

i) Mastère

The "Mastère" course, set up in 1986 by the Confédération des Grandes Ecoles*, awards a "seal of approval" as opposed to a national diploma. It comprises a one-year complementary course which combines tuition with work experience and which follows a 5-year university degree course. This qualification is said to be roughly equivalent to the American Ph.D.

The following table contains data on the number of computer-studies graduates in France (1987).

	QUALIFICATION LEVELS	NUMBERS	TOTAL
General Cert +2	BTS	1 725	4 525
	DUT	2 800	
General Cert +4	Master's	1 450	2 425
	MIAGE	750	
	Master's in Science and Tech. with Computing option	225	
General Cert +5	DESS	400	2 209
	Engineering Colleges	1 809	

* University-level colleges specialising in professional training.

2.2 Existing jobs

There were a wide variety of computing occupations in France in 1988. These depended on such factors as initial training, the profession currently practised, the type of employing firm and salary.

In 1988, the number of computer specialists rose above the 200 000 mark, and this figure is expected to rise to 207 000 (excluding data-entry staff who have no specifically computer-related qualifications) by 1990.

The census carried out in 1982 by the National Institute for Statistics and Economic Studies produced the following breakdown: the total of 176 660 specialists was made up of:

- 38% Engineers and managers
- 6% Technical-sales staff
- 11% Console operators computer-room managers
- 26% Programmers-data preparers
- 19% Operating staff

In the course of the 6 years, since 1982, this breakdown has been subject to many different influences and the whole picture within the profession has changed. No precise information is currently available, so that any attempt to predict trends in the 1990s is inevitably based on guesswork. It should also be noted that the INSEE breakdown does not correspond to the criteria now adopted in all studies of computer-related professions, i.e. a breakdown based on the following four main categories: Systems, Applications, Operating-Maintenance and Sales.

In 1988, 60% of the 200 000 computer specialists (excluding data-entry staff) worked in the computer departments of user firms whilst 25% were employed in computer-service companies. Manufacturers and distributors accounted for only 15%. There is expected to be only a small rise in the total number of specialists employed by 1990, namely a 3.5% increase which will mainly affect the development of service companies, while staffing levels in the more traditional sectors of employment will remain unchanged.

	Total no. employed		1990 forecast	
Software firms	25.50%	51 000	31.00%	64 000
Manufacturers	12.50%	25 000	13.50%	28 000
Users	60.00%	120 000	53.00%	110 000
Distributors	2.00%	4 000	2.50%	5 000
TOTAL		200 000		207 000

2.3 Manpower supply and demand

The "Applications" and "Sales" categories currently offer the largest number of employment opportunities. The "Systems" category remains stable, while the number of openings in "Operating and Maintenance" is showing a comparative decrease.

The APEC (Executive Employment Association) recorded a 63% rise in the number of job vacancies between May 1987 and May 1988; the computer industry continues to lead the field, accounting for 30% of vacancies advertised in the press. Within the space of a year, demand increased by 25% for executives as a whole and by 59% in the case of computer specialists. Most vacancies are in industrial and technical computing, followed by management computing(2).

On the other hand, unemployment has increased among analysts, project managers, department managers, research engineers and systems engineers since, according to the APEC, these jobs would appear to be the most affected by growing number of vacancies.

There is, thus, a widening gap between the qualifications and experience sought by employers and those offered by experienced specialists currently available on the market.

Recruitment is now increasingly geared towards university graduates - as attested by the SARI survey carried out by Séma Sélection in March 1988.
This applies particularly to programmers and analyst/programmers, categories in which recruitment officers are now looking for specialists who have spent four years, rather than just two, in higher education. The proportion of self-taught specialists in this profession (upper secondary school certificate, DEP*, CAP*) fell from 72% in 1978 to 40% in 1988. On the other hand, the number of BTS-holders rose from 26% to 43%. The proportion of students who have spent 4 or 5 years in post-secondary higher education increased from 2% to 17% over the same period; for many of these students, this represents only a career beginning.

In the case of such senior staff as analysts and project managers, the proportion of specialists who have spent 4 years in post-secondary higher education has also increased, thus causing the proportion of self-taught professionals to fall by 13% over a ten-year period.

---

(2) Caillaux B., Peureux H., <u>The computer professions,</u> APEC, "Tomorrow's executives" collection, 1986.

Although the same trend can be observed in the case of managerial positions, it is not yet fully evident, since such positions tend to mark the final stages of a specialist's career. It will still be some time before graduates who have spent 4 or 5 years in higher education reach managerial positions in any significant numbers.

In the "Systems" category, the number of employees educated to General Certificate level (38%) is lower than the number of employees who have spent 4 or 5 years in higher education (42%).

As far as network specialists are concerned, the proportion of engineers is significantly greater (56%). Whilst there are few technicians in this profession (16%), it is still characterized by a large number of self-taught specialists (28%).

The SAR survey confirms the increasing tendency to recruit staff who have spent 4 or 5 years in higher education. It also highlights the gap between the qualifications and experience now sought by employers and the skills offered by experienced specialists currently available on the market.

To sum up, although the overall unemployment rate in the computer industry fell during the first quarter of 1988, unemployment in this sector tends to be structural rather than cyclical. Employer demand is increasingly directed towards specialists who have spent 4 or 5 years in higher education, thus reflecting the growing need for highly qualified staff. In the past, recruiters in the four different categories of the computer industry did not always insist on a high level of initial training, which explains their current quest for skills. A gap exists between the new and the older generation of computer specialists. The latter, insofar as they are less highly qualified, have much greater difficulty in adapting to market demands.

* DEP = Diploma of Professional Studies
* CAP = Certificate of Professional Competence

2.4 Regulatory mechanisms

Employers face a variety of problems with regard to computer professionals. In some professions, specialists are rare and therefore difficult to recruit. Unemployment is low and there is a high level of occupational mobility. Once employed, specialists soon arouse the interest of other firms. The employer's main task is to retain his staff and it is here that the principal factor determining occupational mobility comes into play, namely salaries. Certain professions which are subject to high demand at a given moment and in which there is a shortage of specialists have benefitted from this situation. A few years ago, analyst/programmers were a case in point. Today, however, the fact that salaries have levelled off in this sector is a clear sign that the profession is in decline. Nowadays, it is systems and network specialists who reap the benefits of the difference between company demand and the availability of specialists.

Overall, computer specialists saw their salaries increase at a rate which was more than 4 points higher than the rate of inflation in 1987. This up-grading, which was due entirely to the growth in the computer industry, is itself a useful instrument for regulating staff turnover (10%) in this particular employee category.

3. SOCIAL ASPECTS OF CHANGES IN THE PROFESSIONS

3.1 Qualifications

Programming techniques are constantly developing and are now far more systematized than a few years ago. This fact poses a threat to the know-how of the large number of analyst/programmers who make up the "Applications" category. Only those with the benefit of higher education find it easy to enter other professions (analysts, project managers, etc.) where demand is greater. In this particular group, specialists without previous qualifications, whose training took the form of short intensive courses, are beginning to experience problems both as regards finding work and occupational mobility. The case of analyst/programmers demonstrates the extent to which once highly regarded professions can decline: initially, there is an adequate number of specialists on the market, but during a second phase the profession itself is threatened owing to the speed with which new techniques are developed. The new professions which emerge do not necessarily call for the same skills, thus creating a mismatch between company needs and the experience and qualifications which specialists have to offer.

The speed with which the computer industry is currently developing, is revolutionizing computer manufacture itself: the latest products display an increasingly high level of reliability, thus gradually eliminating the need for maintenance specialists. The category of workers with the lowest qualifications who are responsible for maintenance in the "Operating" group is also in decline.

In spite of the present favourable economic conditions, specialists are experiencing a certain unease, aware that the course of future developments lies beyond their control. They anxiously await new moves on the part of manufacturers in an attempt to identify signs some broader strategy. In actual fact, their concern is merely one symptom of the more general state of anarchy currently affecting the industry. There is no "standard" hardware or software. Certain recent agreements would seem to point to the possibility of a solution the not too distant future. Meanwhile, however, many specialists have turned to artificial intelligence and telecommunications in the belief that these sectors will never be a adversely affected regardless of the hardware or software standards ultimately adopted.

3.2 Mobility

Mobility among computer specialists tends to take one of two possible forms:
- change of activity within a firm
- change of firm, sometimes also accompanied by a change of profession.

The SARI survey conducted by Séma Sélection in 1987 put occupational mobility among computer specialists at 11% between 1981 and 1987. According to the study, mobility within this particular professional category is on a par with occupational mobility among staff in other company deparments.

It is important to note that these average figures conceal other, related phenomena, such as a lower level of mobility in the provinces than in Paris and a higher level in software than in user companies.

Mobility in the computer sector tends to be voluntary. It can be justified by the existence of a highly buoyant market, fuelled by a technology in a constant state of flux.

Mobility is generally upward, i.e. it involves promotion in terms of both functions performed and salary received. Transfer to other professional activities also accounts for a sizeable proportion of these changes.

In 1987, occupational mobility among computer specialists amounted to 10.2% - the lowest rate since 1981, as the following table shows:

	1981-86 Average	1987 Rate
General mobility	12.0%	10.2%
Managerial positions	12.4%	10.1%
Research and design	12.0%	9.9%
Programming	14.2%	11.4%
Operating	10.1%	8.3%
Systems engineers	12.6%	9.9%
Network managers	10.6%	13.2%

(source: Séma Selection survey, 1987)

Although there is evidence of a certain market stabilization, one should note that there are still professionals in which the chronic shortage of specialists coupled with strong market demand produces much higher mobility rates. The current high level of mobility among network specialists (13.2% turnover rate) also existed among applications and systems engineers in the period 1982-84.

Certain types of specialist who, until recently, were in great demand now find themselves with little choice but to change jobs, owing to the annual decrease in the number of openings. This applies particularly to the basic operating jobs - console and computer operators - and to non-technician analyst/programmers trained in a series of intensive short courses, who are now compelled to retrain in order to acquire new skills.

The job market for computer specialists is now achieving a state of overall balance in which the inevitable disappearance of some professions is offset by the emergence of others, thus imposing new demands on the educational system. Technological progress is clearly at the root of this discrepancy.

4. GOVERNMENT POLICIES

France suffered from a shortage of qualified computer specialists in the period 1975-85. The government support plan for the electronics industry (82-86) made it possible to meet this deficiency so that, in 1988, a relative balance has been established between the number of graduates seeking employment and the number of jobs available. Considerable efforts have been made to ensure an adequate annual supply of graduates (the number increased from 4 200 in 1982 to 8 200 in 1986). Nowadays, the problem seems to be rather one of training quality and, hence, qualification levels. The question of whether to extend the two-year post-secondary education course by a further year remains unresolved. It seems unlikely that such an approach, which has already been adopted on a very limited scale in France, could really improve graduate qualifications (since one year is not enough), but it would at least help to bring the French system of technical education into line with other European countries where a three-year period of post-secondary education is much more common. In France, the trend is more towards 5-year post-secondary courses, in an attempt to meet the growing demand of employers for such a level of training.

Among several black spots on the job market, reference can be made to the problem of providing research and lecturing posts in universities and the difficulties involved in adapting course content to suit future professions, the exact details of which are still unclear.

IRELAND

J.F. DINNEEN and M.E.J. O'KELLY
Human Factors Research Unit
University College, Galway

1. Definition of IT professionals

In the present study, Information Technology (IT) professionals are identified primarily by their educational background (predominantly, electronic engineering and computer science) and, to a lesser extent, by their position in the organization: Electronic Data Processing (EDP), Management of Information Systems (MIS) and Software Design. The most reliable statistics available are based on the Irish electronics industry and these will be used to reflect the position of IT professionals in general (1).

2. Labour market

In 1986, Ireland produced 139 computer-science and 347 electronic engineering-graduates. Of those with a first degree degree in computer science, 76 % were employed within a year of graduating, 47 % in Ireland and 29 % abroad. Another 18 % were engaged in research & academic work. Among electronic-engineering graduates, the corresponding percentages were 80 % in employment, 44 % in Ireland and 36 % abroad, with a further 13 % engaged in research & academic work.

Of the 76 % of computer-science graduates who were employed within a year of graduation, 40 % went into Industry (manufacturing industry), 24 % into Commerce (general business, excluding manufacturing) and 8 % into the Professions (mainly consultancy firms). Turning to the corresponding figures for electronic-engineering graduates, of the 80 % engaged in full-time employment, 7 % joined State-Sponsored Bodies (excluding Hospitals), 65 % went into Industry and 2 % into Commerce (2).

---

(1) TCD, Electronic Surveys, Trinity College, Dublin, 1981, 1983 (University College Galway, 1985)

(2) HEA, First destination of award recipients, Higher Education Authority, Dublin, 1986.

3. Development of IT professions

3.1. Skills and working conditions

The only reliable information available on skills and working conditions comes from a number of studies of the electronics industry, carried out by James Wickham, an industrial sociologist from Trinity College, Dublin. In one such study, (Wickham, 1986), he assesses the role of technological education in the industry from the viewpoint of the technically qualified employees themselves.

The electronics sector in Ireland is frequently described as a young industry, and this certainly applies to its skilled manpower. Using Wickham's study as a reference (3), the average IT professional in the Computers sub-sector of the Irish electronics industry is a 28 year old, single male electronics engineer with an annual salary of £IRL 15 200, working for a multinational firm. This average IT professional sees his educational qualification (university degree) as having been very important as regards his application for his present position but not of major relevance to his actual work. He would probably describe his educational knowledge as too theoretical. In terms of career aspirations, he would expect to be working for the same company in three years' time but at least one in three of his peers would have emigrated. If asked the reasons he would probably give for their emigration would be the very high level of personal taxation in Ireland and the fact that their present workload did not adequately tax their level of knowledge - in other words, the work was not interesting enough.

3.2. Careers and professional mobility

With a few exceptions, "high-tech" companies are unable to provide a distinct technical, as opposed to managerial career structure; promotion opportunities, therefore, have to be into management-orientated functions. Thus, while individual career interests tend to be technical, the in-house training provided by companies is usually geared toward management skills. This means that career development depends upon "growing with the company". Unfortunately, in the smaller companies this usually means graduates "learn the ropes in six months and are bored within two years". Emigration is, therefore, attractive to those IT professionals who wish to remain in the technical area.

---

(3) Wickham J., <u>Trends in Employment and Skill in the Irish Electronics Industry</u>, NBST Report, 1986.

4. Government policy

4.1. Restructuring of higher education

Since the publication of the reports of the Commission on Higher Education (1967) and the Steering Committee on Technical Education (1969) in the mid-Sixties, successive governments have launched a number of initiatives aimed at increasing participation in Higher Education, with particular emphasis on Science and Technology.

In the Sixties, the Higher Education Sector consisted mainly of the Universities. The Commission on Higher Education was established in 1960 to enquire into the current state of the sector and to make recommendations. The Commission's report, which was published in 1967, was highly critical of a number of aspects of higher education and made wide-ranging recommendations aimed at improving coordination and planning, achieving higher participation rates, raising academic standards, and increasing emphasis on technological, scientific, and commercial studies. Reactions to the report varied considerably and resulted in notable initiatives being undertaken in areas such as the improvement of entry standards, the provision of student grants and the expansion of the Dublin Colleges of Technology.

In 1969 also, the Higher Education Authority (HEA) recommended the expansion of facilities in a number of universities, including Engineering Schools in both University College, Galway (UCG) and Trinity College, Dublin (TCD). In addition, the HEA called for the establishment of a National Institute of Higher Education in Limerick (NIHEL). In 1975 the National Institute of Higher Education, Dublin (NIHED) was set up.

The growing emphasis on Science and Technology inherent in this re-structuring is best demonstrated by the fact that in 1980, 6 672 students were admitted to colleges of technology compared with 5 513 to university colleges. Even within the university sector itself, the main growth areas have been commerce/business studies and science/engineering.

A number of infrastructural initiatives aimed at increasing industry-education cooperation have also been introduced in the last decade. These include the establishment of incubator factories at UCG, Galway, a technological park in NIHEL, Limerick, and the National Microelectronics Research Centre (NMRC) at UCC, Cork.

4.2. Data Protection Bill

The Data Protection Bill 1987 was presented to the Dail on October 19, 1987. The object of this Bill is to protect the privacy of individuals with regard to computerized personal data. In practice, this legislation will regulate the way in which data about individuals are gathered, processed, retained, and disclosed by computer-users in business, Government agencies, and other bodies.

The Bill provides for the appointment by the Government of a Data Protection Commissioner to supervise the operation of the proposed legislation and to take corrective action where necessary. The new commissioner will have considerable discretion in administering the implementation of this legislation. His most difficult task will be to strike the right balance between protecting the rights of individuals, on the one hand, and being realistic in imposing obligations on businessmen, on the other.

It is too early to comment substantively on the Bill's provision concerning registration. This covers the process which will require computers users to submit certain information about the personal data which they hold, so that this can be used to compile a public register. One of the first tasks of the new Data Protection Commissioner will be to set up this registration process. While such a register is clearly in the public interest, it is essential that a simplified registration process be adopted. It is clear that, if the registration process is too complex, then the legislation will never work in practice.

5. Professional associations and industrial relations

The initials MSF, standing for Manufacturing, Scientific, and Finance, first seen in the general media in February of this year, will become increasingly familiar in the coming months in the world of industrial relations.

MSF is drawn from the well-established white-collar union, the Association of Scientific and Managerial Staffs (ASTMS) and the Technical And Supervisory Section of the Amalgamated Engineering Union (TASS).

In Ireland, MSF will have members in several key industries and services. In banking and insurance, for instance, it will have 14 000 members; in electronics, computing, and manufacturing 6 000; in the semi-State bodies 5 000; in the wider public sector 3 000 and in the National Institutes for Higher Education (NIHED, NIHEL), Vocational Education Committees (VECs), and universities 2 000. A wide variety of smaller sectors will also have MSF representation, from the arts to the voluntary sector. MSF believes that this occupational and industrial coverage will give it a great deal of influence over the development of economic, industrial, and technological policy both in national and local negotiations. TASS and ASTMS already have negotiating rights in some 500 companies and the merger will put an end to wasteful competition. In the public sector, MSF believes that the combined resources of the new union will immensely assist in developing campaigns aimed at improving jobs and conditions.

This merger is also a reflection of the enormous changes that have taken place in both the working environment and technology over the past twenty years. What were once clear differences and distinctions between industries and types of work have diminished and, in some cases, entirely disappeared. Those with similar skills may be working in hospitals, universities, or industry today and in the computer departments of finance houses, in research, or in distribution tomorrow.

ITALY

Information Technology (IT) professionals are widely distributed among specialized enterprises, both in hardware and software production, and user industries in virtually all sectors of the economy. A comprehensive assessment of the working of the particular labour market, in its quantitative and qualitative aspects, is difficult.

1. Definition of IT professions

No official data, sufficiently broken down to provide professional profiles, are available on these categories of workers. The 1981 census data identify only an aggregate group of "analysts and programmers of electronic calculators and computing equipment". This figure did not include top managers and self-employed workers.

Specialized studies do provide more detailed classifications of job descriptions and professional profiles.

The "Guide to the Professions" ("Repertorio delle professioni) recently published by ISFOL (1), the official agency for research on vocational training, lists three groups of IT professionals and provides an outline of the job contents and suggestions for educational and training curricula for young people.

- analyst-programmers
- systems analysts
- assistants to computer users.

---

(1) ISFOL, "Repertorio delle Professioni", Istituto Poligrafico dello Stato, Roma 1987.

The classification adopted by another ISFOL study (2) involves a hierarchy of five levels of responsibility: several job definitions are given for each level:

- general manager of EDP centres or information networks
- professionals with group responsibility
- professionals
- foremen and controllers of operating departments
- operators

In a recent report by CENSIS (3), a public research agency specialising in social studies, professional skills in IT were listed in five functional areas:

- EDP for current administration
- EDP for projects analysis
- user assistance for computing and communication systems
- consultancy for top management
- production

Both these studies stress the changing structure of skill requirements within larger firms. The traditional EDP professional was mainly confined to his specialized department, and essentially responsible for routine systems applications and the coordination of input and output in "batch" operations. The present trend is towards a greater presence of IT specialists and consultants in all other areas of management, where communications networks and office automation systems are becoming increasingly widespread.

---

(2) Butera F., Dalle occupazioni industriali alle nuove professioni, F. Angeli, Milano, 1987.

(3) CENSIS (Centro Studi Investimenti Sociali), Informatica Italia 1986: mercato del lavoro, F. Angeli, Milano, 1987.

2. Labour market

2.1. Output of the education system

Although it is generally admitted that IT skills are mainly acquired through experience, the quality and quantity of the output of the educational system is nonetheless important. In the official education system, the principal curricula leading to IT qualifications are the Degree Courses in Electronic Engineering and Information Sciences at university level, and specialized courses in Informatics ("Periti Informatici") and Accounting with programming ability ("Ragionieri programmatori") at technical- and commercial-secondary-school level.

The latest figures available show an annual output of some 1 500 and 600 graduates in Electronic Engineering and Information sciences respectively. Their number has not increased greatly in recent years, perhaps because of the difficulty of the studies; it has been estimated that the market could absorb 20 to 30 % more graduates than at present each year.

Within public education, 125 out of a total of 944 Industrial Schools were offering a specialization in "Informatica", and 251 out of 1 413 Commercial Schools were providing courses for "Ragionieri programmatori", with a respective output of 6 125 and 8 282 students qualifying at diploma examinations in 1987. This number has been increasing by 6 to 7 % per year since 1981. It must also be remembered that many private enterprises and institutions provide courses and other opportunities for training in IT.

2.2. Employment and demand for IT professionals

A report by CENSIS (Centro Studi Investimenti Sociali) recently (1986) gave an estimate of 400 000 "professional" IT operators (); total labour demand in this field is expected to increase by about 5.5 % per year. These results are extrapolated from a detailed analysis of a small sample and should be considered with caution. Estimating a turnover rate of 5 to 6 %, a potential for approximately 30 000 new vacancies per year might be a realistic figure.

These jobs are divided between computer business and "user" industries; according to a recent estimate, the share of total employment was as follows:

Hardware supplies	13.1 %
Software/Services firms	11.7 %
User sectors	75.2 %

Among user sectors, banking has traditionally provided a major source of demand for IT specialists. A sample survey of 15 major banks reveals that "IT operating costs" represented 9.86 % of total operating expenditure in 1986; the ratio of total staff to IT-related staff, estimated at 25:1, indicates that the latter accounted for 4 % of total employment in this sector.

2.3. Some sectoral case studies

A sample survey (3 937 firms) conducted by the **manufacturing industry** employers' association (CONFINDUSTRIA), shows that there were 643 EDP managers among 15 230 with senior executive duties, and 479 system analysts and 2 011 programmers out of a total of 75 742 technical and clerical staff. The share of total employment accounted for by IT staff is mainly in the 1.5 -2.5 % range in most industrial sectors, with the obvious exception of the computer and office-equipment sector, where the figure is nearly 25 %.

Software houses and other firms specialising in IT services have, however, recently provided the most dynamic source of employment for IT specialists, particularly in the case of higher skills. Software is "labour intensive", and accounted for about a half of the total employment in computer-related businesses in 1987, with a 34 % share of total turnover. The whole sector has been experiencing a growth rate in turnover of more than 20 % per year, with a consistent increase in employment.

The **Public Administration**, both at central and local levels, has always found difficulty in recruiting IT specialists, because of the unattractive salaries in public employment. For important projects and for many higher skills, the State has to seek the support and advice of "external" firms. Whilst some firms, such as those in the FINSIEL group of companies, are controlled by the State as the majority shareholder, they are not subject to the rigidities of the public employment system. They often act as the privileged supplier of consultants for systems and software implementation. Detailed figures on IT staffing levels and systems expenditures within Central Government and its agencies are regularly published by the State Procurement Office at the Treasury.

2.4. Labour market regulation

A variety of contractual forms and the coexistence of dependent and independent labour, with a high rate of mobility among firms and tasks, seem to characterize the upper IT specialist brackets. This makes their specific labour market particularly unsuitable for analysis in terms of traditional industrial relations categories.

Reporting on a specialized study (4), we identified three typical work-relationship patterns:

a) "consultants", i.e. senior professionals with a formally independent status, who are, however, often "tied" to a single firm or organization through "exclusive work" contracts, explicitly or implicitly excluding the possibility of simultaneous cooperation with competing firms;

b) "dependent labour", which is still prevalent in user industries and larger hardware firms, and for which working conditions are regulated by sectoral collective agreements; however, except for lower categories of operators, collective agreements define only minimum working conditions and standard benefits (such as holidays, sick pay, etc.), with additional earnings being negotiated above this level;

c) "temporary detachment", called "bodyrent" in the jargon, where a software house or other specialized firm "lends" the client firm, a professional worker for a limited period in order to help with the implementation of new systems or to pass on expertise to local staff; cases were also reported of staff "exchanges" between specialized IT firms. The formally autonomous state of many "consultants" facilitates mobility and informal contracts; beyond these forms of organized labour, there are also a number of genuinely independent "free-lancers" working individually or in small partnerships.

---

(4) Della Rocca G., <u>La formazione del rapporto di lavoro nelle attivita di produzione del software</u>, mimeo, Milano, 1987.

d) "Free-lancers" or professional partnerships: from survey data, many local units in the software and IT services sector appear to be very small. Instances of partnerships and associations of professionals retaining their independent status are also frequent. Independent labour is found at all levels of specialization and skill content from the "free-lance" programmer helping with the routine tasks of small establishments (e.g. shopkeepers), to top levels of sophisticated consultancy. Independent work may also be a part-time or "second-job" option of qualified persons already in secure posts (e.g. academic, or other research and teaching positions).

3. Changing professional profiles

3.1. Skills and work organization

The impact of IT within the organizational structure of the user firm has increased in recent years from a marginal, although important role (the specialized EDP centre) to affect all the internal (administrative, commercial, R&D, etc.) functions of the firm (5). The average age of a specialized EDP department in larger organizations, such as major banks and industrial enterprises or public-administration departments is now about 20/25 years. However the development of IT on the basis of diffused network systems has reduced the role of the central EDP department and of "batch" data processing in it, to the benefit of systems distributed data and information input and processing systems. The availability of standardized application packages has, in some cases, reduced the requirement for the "in-house" production of software and other programming input. On the other hand, the great expansion of specialized software houses and other "service" firms is indicative of the trend towards increased outside purchasing of IT-related functions and skills by user organizations.

The EDP centre must then progress from the general performance of standard "jobs" to become a "service centre" for the solution of problems within the whole network. Thus, it appears that while some specialized EDP staff remain "dedicated" to the control and management of existing technology and standard operations, other staff will be specifically assigned to systems expansion in innovative organizations.

---

(5) This section is mainly inspired by R. Bellini, G. Franchina: "Come cambiano le professioni informatiche", in "Management e informatica", Aprile 1987.

A certain selection between "routine" and "innovative" members of staff may occur. Often, "problem-solving" or "consulting" tasks are farmed out to specialist firms, software houses etc.; higher skills may then be increasingly concentrated among these specialized groups.

In conclusion, although the gradual acquisition of skills from partial programming tasks to "system" responsibility still enables motivated personnel to progress, "critical" conditions of increasing demand not sufficiently matched by qualified applicants, seem to exist only in the upper reaches of the profession, if at all.

3.2. Work contracts and careers

It is very difficult to obtain information on earning levels. Within "user enterprises", the dependent worker specializing in IT does not normally receive a job-specific contract, but is formally covered by the contract applicable to the industrial (or service) category of the employing firm.

New staff holding a University degree are normally at level 6 on being hired (most contracts in Italy distinguish 8 levels or salary classes with corresponding job profiles) Career progress leads to the 8th, or top level; further advancement implies passage to "managers" ("dirigenti") status. In this case, national collective agreements with trade-unions are no longer relevant and salaries and other working conditions are individually agreed with the employer. The specialist with secondary-school education will normally reach the 7th level as a senior programmer.

The greatest difference between the public and private sectors lies in the fact that while salaries are rigidly fixed in the former, in the latter local bargaining, either collective or individual, brings effective earnings well above the minimum standard set by national collective agreements. Case studies of workers in software and IT services have shown that dependent workers earn about 50 to 60 % more than the contractual standards.

A skilled IT professional will attempt to improve his career and earnings through "external" and "internal" mobility between and within firms, often involving a change from dependent to independent status. However, the essential condition is possession of sufficient training and "on-the-job" skills. This normally requires a period of at least three years "on-the-job" experience in a large organization after leaving school.

It is generally agreed that the highest earners are "top consultants"; only at the highest managerial level, may dependent work produce comparable earnings. The estimated market value of a particular skill (for example, Lire 200 000 per hour of work by a senior analyst) is also often used as a reference datum when negotiating individual managers' salaries.

3.3. Professional mobility

The mobility, in terms of IT specialist firms, posts and contractual arrangements is generally considered to be high. They seek progress in their careers and earnings through "external" as well as "internal" mobility, often involving a transition from dependent to independent status. The essential precondition is that of having acquired initial skills and on-the-job training for at least two or three years after the end of formal education.

Turnover shows great variations among specific categories of workers, being particularly high in "critical" brackets; the following table gives the distribution of voluntary departures in a sample of dependent EDP centre staff on the basis of their professional qualification.

After an initial period of acquisition of "on-the-job" training, anlysts/programmers have a high propensity to move on. This is because of the reduced possibility of increasing their earnings, unless they obtain a higher qualification or achieve managerial status; in fact, they will have reached level 7 in the contractual classification, which is normally the upper limit for technical workers without a university qualification. At that point, economic improvement depends on the individual bargaining of "extra-contractual" or "merit" earnings with an employer, or with successful acquisition of an independent professional status. Thus, attempts will be made to improve mobility and status, although it may frequently prove impossible to increase existing wage levels.

3.4. Training and retraining requirements

Continuous updating of skills is essential in a sector characterized by technological innovation and keen competition. The larger computer firms (mainly, IBM Italia, Olivetti, Honeywell Information Systems (Italia)) play an important role as organizers of training for their own and clients' staff. A case-study of Olivetti reveals that training sessions are constantly organized at four different levels: "school-leavers", "potential managers", "middle management" and "senior executives". ELEA, a specialized firm within the Olivetti group, has specific responsibility for these activities.

Specialized consulting firms organize training sessions for outside professionals. About 39 % of software houses analyzed in a survey hired out "training consultants" as a part of their market activity.

Professional trends are extremely difficult to evaluate in a dynamic environment such as the IT labour market. A specification of job profiles may produce very detailed classifications; however, higher levels of professional ability may imply a "systemic vision" and flexibility among tasks rather than narrower specialization. The traditional working environment of IT specialists, that of the EDP department, had a rather stable hierarchy, and a fixed career structure (from part-programmer to systems manager); the diffusion of IT to cover all the activities of complex organizations is changing the role of the IT specialist from the management of quantitative data in the EDP centre to "problem-solving" throughout the whole information network.

4. Government policy

No specific agency, either at central government or regional level, intervenes to influence the labour market for IT professionals. In practice, the mobility of IT professionals does not depend on public employment exchanges. In terms of surveys of the labour market and student guidance, the national or regional "Monitoring Services for the Professions" identify changing IT-related skills and provide advice on educational curricula.

The main difficulty affecting the project for the "automation of the Public Administration" is still the shortage or early departure of staff attracted by high salaries in the private sector. The existing legislation and regulations on public employment do not allow IT specialists to be distinguished from other personnel holding equivalent educational qualifications or to receive preferential treatment as regards salary or other conditions.

5. Professional organizations and industrial relations

Given the extremely "individualistic" behavior of these specialized workers, the role of trade-unions or other collective organizations is minimal. A specialist survey states: "Collective agreements define the patterns of working conditions only for administrative and data-processing staff". In the case of more senior staff, collective agreements only define minimum earnings and working conditions.

The only associations specifically for IT specialists are mainly of a scientific character; they organize conferences and seminars which, in addition to scientific exchanges, provide an occasion for discussing matters of common interest to the category.

The informal circulation of information on "average" earnings and conditions is encouraged on these occasions. Technical journals and IT supplements in other periodicals also help to disseminate information.

These sources also act as informal "labour exchanges" through the advertisement of vacancies by firms and availability by workers.

In conclusion, the IT labour market can be said to be somewhat removed from the wider context of industrial organization or employee/management relations.

LUXEMBOURG

Jeff KINTZELE
Research Centre of the Société Luxembourgeoise
Luxembourg

The main problem in any attempt to gauge the state of the job market for computer specialists in Luxembourg lies in the almost total lack of information. There is a marked shortage of statistics, both on the educational system (newly qualified graduates) and on employment.

The most salient feature of the Luxembourg job market for computer professionals is the considerable discrepancy between the number of job applicants and the number of vacancies; at every level of training, the latter is significantly higher than the former. Hence, the widespread employment of foreign workers in an effort to compensate for the national shortage.

Only one study - a forecast - has been conducted on the subject. It dates from 1981 and the figures have never been updated. It was designed to identify the need for computer specialists until year 1986.

1. DEFINING "COMPUTER PROFESSIONALS"

In Luxembourg, computer specialists are most commonly defined on the basis of their qualifications. It should, however, be pointed out from the start that the absence of statistics makes it difficult to provide an accurate picture of the situation.

The official statistics compiled by the Central Service of Statistics and Economic Studies (STATEC) do not include a category for computer specialists.

1.1 Degrees in computing

One of the most notable aspects of Luxembourg's education policy is the widespread opportunity, and in some cases the necessity, for study abroad, particularly in Belgium, France and Germany. University education is always acquired abroad.

Upon completing his secondary education, any student wishing to pursue computer studies in Luxembourg can either enroll in the "applied computing" section of the Higher Institute of Technology (IST), or in a short course of advanced management studies at the Luxembourg University Centre (CUL). The former leads to an engineering degree (involving a 3-year post-secondary course) which is geared towards computer hardware and electronics rather than software. The latter leads to a degree which is similar to the Belgian degree in computing (upper secondary school certificate + 2 years in higher education) and is geared towards analysis and management computing.

The Federation of Employees in the private sector provides continuing education courses which, since 1971, have included an introductory course in computing. For the academic year 1988/89, the computers course was modified at second-year level, in order to take greater account of user requirements. The course is now subdivided to provide four specific options:

- large-system programming (COBOL)
- micro-computer programming (DBASE)
- applied micro-computing
- computer analysis

These courses have enjoyed a certain degree of success. Some private schools also offer introductory courses in computing, particularly word processing for secretaries, although precise data are not available.

A notable feature of the Luxembourg education system is its openness to foreign influence. In the case of university education, study abroad is actually compulsory.

It would be impossible to list all the different options currently available to Luxembourg students. Given the national lack of computer specialists, there is no problem when it comes to comparing and recognising the various diplomas. All of which tends to compound the confusion surrounding the number of Luxembourge students of information technology (IT) (at whatever level) and the variety of qualifications.

Moreover, it is impossible to establish the number of students returning to Luxembourg to work as computer professionals. It is generally believed, however, that the number who choose to remain abroad, particularly those who possess a university degree, is quite high.

1.2 Classifying the professions

The Ministry of National Education entrusted an advisory Committee with the task of studying the problems raised by the development of micro-electronics and information technology at post-primary level and in continuing vocational training. In 1982, the Committee submitted its report to the Ministry, based on a survey of the job market for computer professionals. The study included a table showing the various types of computer professionals, the different functions performed and the basic training courses available both at the time of the study (1981) and in the medium-term future (1986).

The above-mentioned study represents the only attempt to assess the job market for computer professionals in Luxembourg. We will begin by outlining the various categories defined in the study. Since there is no explanation of the methodology adopted, the scientific value of the study cannot be assessed. The representativeness of the data quoted must also be considered doubtful.

The study begins with a breakdown relating to initial training. The authors distinguish 6 categories:

- <u>university studies:</u> the study and design of applications, data bases, networks and operating/analysis systems.

- <u>short university courses:</u> analysis and programming.

- <u>technical-college courses:</u> programming, maintenance.

- <u>post-secondary studies:</u> programming, operating.

- <u>technical training</u> or <u>commercial and business college studies:</u> programming, operating, maintenance.

- five years of <u>post-primary study:</u> operating, programming.

Ten **professional categories**, corresponding to the actual functions performed within firms, are identified and described as follows:

- Research and design - applications
- Research and design - data bases, networks and operating systems.
- Systems and program design
- Programming
- Operating
- Organization and liaison with user departments
- Computer engineering
- Technical maintenance
- Technical and business-oriented functions
- Other computer functions.

2. MAIN CHARACTERISTICS OF THE JOB MARKET

In the absence of precise quantitative data on the job market for computer professionals in Luxembourg, this report will be confined to the principal.

2.1 Supply and demand

The Luxembourg market is characterized by a marked shortage of computer professionals. Luxembourge graduates have no difficulty in finding jobs and the shortage of manpower within the country is made up by foreign workers, especially from frontier regions.

The shortage is most noticeable in the upper reaches of the education system, particularly in the case of designers and systems engineers. Very often, foreign consultancy firms are assigned specific tasks in this field. Demand for analysts continues to grow while the need for programmers has tended to level off. Here, as elsewhere, data-entry operators are beginning to disappear.

In the case of newly created jobs (highly qualified salesmen, data-base managers, etc.) demand for manpower largely outstrips supply.

2.2 Existing jobs

The Advisory Committee of the Ministry of National Education carried out a survey into existing jobs (1981) and the prospects for 1986.

In 1981, the study recorded 1 202 employees working in computer departments. This figure was based on information supplied by 78 firms which replied to the Advisory Committee's questionnaire. Analysis of the information revealed a probable increase of 344 in the number of employees by 1986. In other words, approximately 70 new jobs are created in the computer industry each year.

On the basis of this study, the breakdown of employees in 1981 was as follows (1986 forecast in brackets): university graduates: 14.31% (16.3%); students having completed short, post-secondary courses: 8.23% (13.07%); technical-college graduates: 5.16% (7.31%); school-leavers: 32.03% (26.78%); technicians or business-schools graduates: 7.52% (12.87%); students having completed five years of post-primary study: 32.70% (23.67%).

This study is not immune to the various difficulties associated with any forecast. Since the report makes little reference to its methodological basis, it cannot be evaluated. It is most unfortunate that no attempt was made to check the statistics or repeat the study. Nevertheless, in view of the absence of more reliable data, the study at least provides an outline of existing trends on the job market for computer professionals.

2.3 Breakdown of jobs by sectors

There are no published surveys relating IT professions to economic sectors or company size. Nevertheless, one may safely assume that the majority of specialists are employed in the services sector (banks, insurance companies, consultancy firms etc.).

2.4 Recruitment strategies

Students who manage to complete their course of study at the IST or the shorter course at the University Centre of Luxembourg find employment straight away. Generally speaking, Luxembourg graduates with degrees in computing have no difficulty finding jobs.

The chronic shortage of computer specialists explains Luxembourg's heavy dependence on foreigners (estimated ratio: 2 Luxembourg nationals for 10 foreigners). The advertisement of vacancies is highly significant in this respect. There is an increasing tendency to publish directly in foreign newspapers such as the "Républicain Lorrain" (France) or "Le Soir" (Belgium), since all too often advertisements in the national press go unanswered.

2.5 Salaries

No accurate information is currently available on salaries. In certain sectors, the existence of a collective agreement leaves little room for manoeuvre. Small and medium-sized firms, on the other hand, are governed by market forces. State institutions and some larger firms offer computer bonuses (particularly in respect of preparatory work undertaken outside normal office hours).

THE NETHERLANDS

Dirk VAN DER WERF

Maastricht

In 1985 the Higher Education Committee on the Informatics Plan (Commissie Hoger Onderwijs Informaticaplan) published its "CHIP" report (1). This report set the standard for forecasting the needs for trained informatics experts in the Netherlands and furnished policy-makers with the information required to plan the educational structure in this field of knowledge and know-how.

The main conclusions of this Committee are:

- In 1990 there will be an annual structural demand for 7 600 information technology (IT) specialists with higher education; this annual demand will grow to 8 900 by 1995.

- All those in higher education who leave university by 1995 should have sufficient knowledge of the technological applications of informatics in their scientific or technical discipline.

- The demand for specialized teachers in higher education will increase to 1 300 theoretical specialists and 900 technical specialists by 1990.

- The infrastructure of higher education should be gradually supplemented, a call already made in comparable reports on further education and computer facilities for institutes of higher education.

As will be seen below, the above-mentioned figures have been updated and discrepancies in supply and demand seem to be developing somewhat less alarmingly - under the influence of market forces ? - than the CHIP forecasts would suggest. Nevertheless, shortages of qualified personnel do seem likely to affect the future expansion of electronic and optronic informatics.

---

(1) CHIP, Eindrapport (Final Report), Commissie Hoger Onderwijs Informaticaplan, The Hague, 1986

1. Definition of "IT professionals"

In its report, the CHIP-Committee drew a clear distinction between:

(a) Specialists trained in the basic IT theory, with a formal expertise in data-processing systems - hardware and software, methods and data - but without specialized knowledge of specific applications and their use (Dutch: informatici);

(b) Specialists trained in the application of informatics by contrast with (a) a great many different specializations are possible in this case (Dutch: informatie-kundigen).

This distinction is clearest for personnel with higher qualifications. Those taking up employment directly after leaving further education are generally required to work on applications. Specific training for these persons is directly related to their function in the organization. Fewer and fewer people now qualify as autodidacts given the increasing demand for expertise. Learning on the job is almost exclusively complemented by specialized training and courses.

The NGI (the Dutch Informatics Association) published complete descriptions (2) of 26 jobs classified under the headings of (a) systems design, (b) support, (c) processing and (d) systems use. These definitions are related to positions in the organization.

The NGI list of job descriptions excludes data entry as an IT function. This is logical, as data entry hardly calls for informatics expertise. In addition, as has already been pointed out, it is becoming more and more difficult to work one's way to the position of an informatics specialist even at a lower level without specialized training.

Not listed are:

- high-level IT specialists, who are not part of an information organization, such as IT researchers, equipment developers, teachers, accountants and commercial officials;

- IT service officials who are not IT professionals: VDU desk operators, data-entry typists, word-processing typists, etc.;

---

(2) NGI, <u>Functies in de Informatica</u>, Rapport van de Werkgroep Functie-ordening van het Nederlands Genootschap voor Informatica (Functions in Informatics, Report of the Working Group Function-ordening of the Dutch Association for Informatics), third edition, Amsterdam 1988.

- managers of IT departments, who are not primarily engaged in professional IT activities;

- The main areas of new industrial automation functions are:

  (a) production automation:

  - computer-aided manufacturing (CAM)

  - process control

  - computer-aided logistics

  Product automation applications mostly involve specialized decision-making computers that react to non-digital sensor signals and directly control production.

  (b) design and control operations:

  - computer-aided design (CAD)

  - expert systems

  The systems in this group largely fulfil a stand-by function for design and control. CAD is used to improve design efficiency and produce patterns ready for use in the automated production system. In expert systems, the codified expertise of experienced technicians is collected and made available as a source of reference for less-experienced operators.

  (c) product automation

  - embedded systems

  Embedded systems combine both of the above-mentioned procedures into a fully-integrated automated production system.

  These production-automation applications are a fairly recent feature of many industrial plants in the Netherlands and are still in the process of full development. Functions in production automation are therefore subject to rapid change and difficult to define in job descriptions.

2. The labour market

Latest reports confirm that the great demand on the labour market for informatics engineers and information experts has been easing recently. There are a number of reasons for this development, of which the most important are probably:

- on the supply side: the increasing output of the higher-education system as a consequence of a reduction in the number of years required to complete the academic curriculum: a complete vintage is now squeezed on to the labour market;

- on the demand side: the so-called automation of information is replacing the time-consuming process of traditional programming (using COBOL and related languages), thus making redundant the traditional programmer who uses these languages.

Nonetheless, at a symposium held in Utrecht in September last year, the Royal Institute of Engineers concluded that this continuing shortage of specialists in electronics and telematics was due to the existing divide between the theoretical character of higher education and the practical nature of - in this particular case - telecommunications. Electronics and telecommunications are not very popular among students, and the limited number of successful students easily find their way to industry and industrial salaries.

This situation is giving rise to considerable gaps in the educational system. There is a kind of a vicious circle creating or maintaining qualification gaps in relation to other countries.

2.1. Output of the education system

Higher education is the main source of the education system. Other sources are regular further education and intermediate-level vocational training programmes.

Estimates for 1985-6 quoted in the above-mentioned CHIP Report suggest that the workforce of information technology professionals in the Netherlands is/was about 85 000 persons, if calculated on a full-time basis (arbeidsjaren). The definition excludes data entry. About 40 000 of these have higher-education qualifications (HBO-level or University). The remaining 45 000 have either further- or basic-education qualifications supplemented by complementary courses or self-acquired skills.

For "informatici" - specialists in the theoretical side of informatics - an estimate of 522 successful students leaving university is given for 1990. The number of students at that date is put at 4 088.

For "informaticakundigen", students in applied informatics, capacity for the 1984-85 academic year was estimated at 180 students.

The four vocational-training programmes mentioned below are joint ventures involving Government (Ministries of Social Affairs, Education and Economic Affairs) and Industry.

The ISI-Project (Instroomproject Informatieberoepen or IT Professionals Inflow Project) provides 9 months training for people leaving the education system and seeking additional training as microcomputer assistants or application programmers and the like in order to find a job. The education level is basic or intermediate. The annual target output is approximately 5 000, and the Programmes which began in September 1985, run for 3 to 5 years.

The PION-Project (IT Training Project) involves 100 days' (re)training of unemployed persons with higher education for informatics jobs. The annual output target is 300 and the Programmes - starting in 1986 - will last for 3 years.

The NIIO National Make-up Programme for IT Training provides additional instruction for people already working in the IT sector who are in need of further training or an updating of their knowledge and know-how. The course length is flexible. Target: approx. 7 500 in five years. Programme duration: 5 years starting in 1986.

The ACSI'85 Computer Services Action Plan for Industry is designed to provide training in programming or systems analysis for people with higher education, whether or not they are already employed. The scheduled annual capacity is 500. Duration 3 years, starting 1985.

2.2. Employment of IT professionals

The Automatiseringsstatistiek 1988 gives estimates of the office workforce up to 1988 for the private sector and up to 1986 for the public sector (3).

---

(3) CBS, Automatiseringsstatistieken, Industriële Automatisering 1984-1986, Central Bureau of Statistics, The Hague, 1987. CBS, Overheidssector 1983-1984, The Hague, 1986. CBS, Particuliere Sector 1986, The Hague, 1988.

Personnel in office automation:

Year	Private sector	Public sector
1983	59 200	9 800
1984	n.a.	10 400
1985	66 545	11 100
1986	75 750	11 500
1987	85 073	n.a.
1988	90 224	n.a.

The number of vacancies in the private sector in 1986 is estimated to have been 4 614. This, and other figures for 1986, are broken down by branch and size of the undertaking. The number of vacancies in the public sector in 1983 was 250 and in 1985 270.

2.3. Case studies in respect of IT professions

Recently the leading research organizations (ITS, Nijmegen, Institute for Applied Sociology, IVA, Tilburg, Institute for Labour Market Issues, Leiden, Werkgroep Arbeidsvraagstukken en Welzijn) have been engaged in case-study research into IT-activities, although the results are not yet available. The available information is given below.

A project on Office Automation in the Services Sector (4) was sponsored by OSA, Organization for Strategic Labour Market Research. It is a pilot project using the methodology developed in the Georgia Institute of Technology, Atlanta, USA, in the Dutch context (5).

Principal conclusions: automation always correlates with a decrease in employment under the conditions assumed in the study. According to the most likely forecasts, and by comparison with 1987 levels, total employment in the sector will have decreased by 2 % to 9 % in 1990 and by 3 % to almost 13 % in the year 2000. Employment levels will be reduced most for secretaries and least for middle managers. According to the minimum forecasts, the decrease will be about 7 % for all groups. In the year 2000, the minimum reductions will be 4.5 % for middle managers, 9 % for professionals/staff and 11% for secretaries. The maximum forecast quotes figures that

---

(4) Zanders H.L.G., Willems A.G., Office Automation in the Services Sector, CPI/KUB Tilburg, september 1987.

(5) Roessnes D., Porter A., The Impact of Office Automation on Clerical Employment, 1985-2000, Georgia Tech Team, 1985

are less extreme than the most likely predictions, because of the compensating effects of time-saving on the workload. The decrease in 1990 is lowest (2%) for middle managers, 4% for professionals & staff and 7% for secretaries. For the year 2000, the corresponding figures are 3 %, 5 % and 11 %. There will be a reduction in employment levels in all groups.

2.4. Labour market regulation processes

Although it always appears easy to attribute particular developments to the effects of market-regulation processes, it is generally very difficult to prove. If particular phenomena or trends are classified in this section, this is not done in absolute certainty of the market's influence.

We will mention three trends in this connection: (a) the automation of automation, (b) the more frequent use of job contracts and (c) the increasing information content of traditional professions. Finally, there is the uncertain influence of salaries, which are mostly higher than in other sectors requiring comparable levels of education and experience.

(a) The automation of automation. The use of modern complex languages is easing the work of programming and systems analysis and leading to the displacement of those traditionally doing these jobs. Extensive writing in COBOL and more advanced languages is gradually being taken over by software generators.

The discernible result is a reduced demand for the services of programmers and systems analysts. If this trend becomes generalized, specialized informatics personnel with basic and intermediate qualifications will continue to be displaced in the future. There would appear to be two consequences, namely:

- an increased demand for people with traditional skills supplemented by an informatics component; and

- improved opportunities for more highly qualified specialists.

(b) The job contract system. The number of secondments and job contracts (employment contracts for the limited period in which a particular task has to be done) has clearly increased in recent years, particularly in the case of such intellectual activities as programming, systems analysis and other automation operations, although the level is now stabilizing. Though these trends can be seen as part and parcel of flexibilization of the employment contract system, it is the scarcity of well-trained and experienced specialists that stimulates and confirms it. In fact, these specialists are too specialized and too expensive to be permanently employed in the jobs in question by smaller and medium-sized employers. Flexible contracts allow a more efficient input of specialized labour and thus tend to reduce slack.

On the other hand the trend provides opportunities for people with special abilities and skills to be employed effectively in the thinner informatics markets.

Secondment does occur when employees of software houses or consultancies are put to work in automation, etc, or other industrial activities, whereas job contracts appear when free-lancers are engaged by software houses and others to do special jobs. Experts on employment contract legislation have expressed the view that a need for tripartite contract bargaining is felt in cases involving secondment, under which the "worker" as the party between the employer (software house) and out-contractor (to whom he is seconded) is given a greater say in all matters. In the case of free-lance job contracting, this gap is gradually being filled by broker houses specializing in mediating between free-lancers and employing firms.

(c) The information content of traditional activities: the taking-over of specialized work by trained traditional professionals, who can cope with tasks made easier by the above-mentioned process of automation. Thus, specialists with deficient education or training are forced out from two sides: by the better educated and by non-specialists. From a labour market viewpoint, this can be described as a process of rationalization, reflecting reduced demand in terms of numbers of information technology professionals.

A recent investigation by HELIVIEW quotes salary levels corresponding to the principal functions. These are averages. Variations are not insignificant: differences of 30% are no exception. As a general rule, business pays significantly better than government. The salary structure Hfl per year is as follows:

30 000 - 39 999: operator

40 000 - 49 999: data manager, systems coordinator, junior salesman, programmer analyst, operations research analyst, network coordinator, help-desk officer, first operator, production analyst, job controller

50 000 - 59 999:   information analyst, trainer adviser, data-base manager, software librarian, systems programmer, network specialist, space manager, microcomputer adviser, microcomputer assistant

60 000 - 69 999:   senior sales adviser, EDP-auditor, adviser/methods and techniques, systems engineer, coordinator info supply, systems analyst

70 000 - 89 000:   senior consultant, adviser info supply

90 000 + over: sales manager

3. Social aspects and trends

3.1. Work organization

Though some attempts are now being made to distinguish different forms of IT work organization, it is of course clear that every organization has its own shape and there is no such thing as the "typical" or "best" work organization for such activity. The differences in product range, the organization of production and/or development and technology are too great to allow conclusions to be drawn with regard to a general tendency.

This does not alter the fact that most organizations and industrial relations are influenced by labour-market tensions and are constantly changing. Without being complete, the following list of trends may be mentioned:

(a) IT activities are being increasingly decentralized under the influence of a number of factors, the most important of which might be the opportunities offered by telecommunications. This physical separation does not imply a concomitant decentralization of decision-making.

(b) Professional mobility is great, as can normally be expected in a sellers' market. This results in all kinds of work relationships that are covered by normal employment contracts. (Compare the earlier comments on job contracts.)

(c) Careers are changing. The NGI has conducted research into the career chains developing between jobs, given skills, particular qualification requirements and opportunities for acquiring in-work experience. The authors of the report "Functies in de Informatica" are very well aware of the impossibility of identifying a detailed career pattern. Nonetheless, they have been able to give indications of the most logical forms of job transfer in new organizations.

(d) Professional levels of education, training and experience are being upgraded. The NGI report gives the new requirements for IT professionals.

Professionalism is increasing. Educational requirements and job standards are now higher than some years ago.

Next to education and experience, the IT professional is increasingly dependent on social and intellectual skills to qualify for his job. The NGI-group listed these skills. The group is aware of the imprecise nature of such an approach which should not be taken to indicate absolute requirements. The extent to which these requirements are fully valid also depends on applications, the organizational structures used and the placing and responsibilities of jobholders therein.

(e) Investment in training is increasing. The business sector has become a major investor in the training of personnel in automation and informatics. A survey conducted in 1986 by the Heliview Marketing Services consultancy shows that 28% of all undertakings with more than 10 employees had personnel trained by specialized agencies.

The average outlay in that year was Hfl 11 735 for an average of 34 days' training 4.21 employees. Thus, the average trainee received 8 days' instruction at a cost of somewhat less than Hfl 2 800 or at Hfl 350 per day.

The survey indicated an average increase in outlay to Hfl 14 400 in 1987, mainly owing to the growing numbers of trainees.

(f) The use of courseware in the vocational training of personnel is becoming more and more interesting for the business sector. A major problem remains in that the supply of educational software is still insufficient in terms of quality and quantity. The present generation of software, including the expert systems used for this purpose, still lacks the necessary in-depth knowledge of the subject and relies too much on drill and practice. Training software in general still needs a significant amount of development, and, if imported, requires adaptation to be usable in the national linguistic and cultural context.

3.2. Women and new technology

Under this heading, reference may be made to the work of the Social Science Faculty in Leiden, in particular the working party "Arbeidsvraag stukken en Welzijn" (A&W).

In 1986, research carried out at the request of the FNV union and the Ministry of Social Affairs and Employment was published on Women's work in industry and automation (6). This research focussed on technological innovation in industry and related issues; options and opportunities for women; three case studies in industrial plants; forecasts of likely changes and qualitative and quantitative estimates of their implications for women's employment.

4. Government policies

The Government is very active in promoting education and training in order to increase supply, by means of programmes and similar measures. On the other hand, it is handicapped by a politically determined salary policy, that thwarts its own recruitment and, worse still, recruitment within the educational system.

By creating obstacles to its own recruitment, government lacks the necessary expertise to complete IT or automation projects successfully. As a result, projects fail and need to be repeated. This absorbs capacity, that could have been put to better use.

In the education system the main problem concerns teachers, since potential candidates prefer the more attractive remuneration levels available in the business sector. This raises the burning question of where the future teachers of IT professionals are to be found.

The labour exchanges fulfil a useful role as regards the labour market for IT personnel. Apart from their normal task of matching supply to jobs, where the best prospects are those of school leavers, now that almost all employers require at least some experience of computers, the labour exchanges direct those looking for jobs, but lacking the necessary IT skills to the available (re)training schemes. They regulate access to subsidized courses for unemployed persons, who have the chance of getting a job, the cost of which is shared by the labour exchange and the prospective employer.

---

(6) Trommel W.A., van Dam R., <u>Vrouwen, industrie en automatisering</u> (Women, Industry and Automation), Industriebond FNV (FNV reeks arbeid en technologie), Amsterdam, 1986.

In this connection, reference should also be made to the annual "job fairs" for IT professionals, jointly organized by the labour exchanges and the business sector.

5. Professional associations and industrial relations

Industrial relations in the fields of informatics and automation in the Netherlands can generally be characterized by three attitudes: informality, individualism and belief in market forces. This has to do with the strong position of the well-qualified specialist. Those whose qualifications become insufficient through educational shortcomings or outdated experience - for instance those who have not learned to master the newest languages - are condemned to leave the market. Organizations to protect such people do not exist, because they have not been created.

5.1. Professional groups and associations

The NGI, Dutch Informatics Association, is the leading association of IT professionals in the Netherlands. It is organized in sections by specialized subject and also by a regional structure. The NGI seeks to bridge the present gap between research and application. One of the sections of this active and highly professional association, SAIA, is concerned with the social aspects of informatics.

5.2. Unions and Collective Agreements for IT professionals

In general, information technology professionals in the Netherlands are not organized in Unions. There are no specialized Unions of any importance in the profession and, according to the available sources, the number of members of service-sector unions who are information technology specialists is insignificant.

Nor are there special collective agreements for IT professionals in the Netherlands. This category of worker is formally covered by the collective agreements in force in the sector or company of employment.

However, the social position of automation personnel in its relation to management is generally far from weak. On the contrary, EDC and automation departments are frequently strongholds of initiative and influence within the company, based on specialized knowledge and know-how. At least, this is the conclusion of a recent survey by ICON Nederland (International Computer Occupations Network).

5.3. Professional ethics

The recently created VRI, the Dutch Association of Registered Informaticians, is promoting professional responsibility in informatics. The association's code of conduct gives a description of good professional behaviour. This code states inter alia:

- statements, actions and decisions of members must be in conformity with professional standards;

- members will ensure the confidentiality and integrity of data;

- members will avoid the abuse, or unprofessional use, of resources and systems;

- members should be aware of the possible impact of their actions within their organizations.

Membership of the VRI, which was created in 1984, is growing.

PORTUGAL

Luís TADEU ALMEIDA
Instituto Superior Técnico
Lisboa

1. Definition of "IT professionals"

The classifications and data used were taken from the "Personnel Tables" the enterprises send yearly to the Ministry of Employment and Social Security and are organized according to the professional categories shown in the IRC (Instrumento de Regulamentação Colectiva) in which all workers are included. Through the respective functional content, an equivalence table is prepared which allows the conversion of the categories mentioned into the present CNP (Classificação Nacional de Profissões, National Classification of Professions) (1).

For the sake of clarity, these professions were classified in four groups: Analysts, Programmers, Operators and Data Entry Operators.

It should be stressed that, of the roughly 500 IRC categories which existed at the end of 1986, the 199 shown in the March Personnel Tables covered professional categories with informatics functions, though only 49 related to IT professionals strictly speaking.

The number of informatics personnel given in the QP/86 (Personnel Tables) - 9347 - , is equivalent to approximately 0.5 % of the total number of employees (TPCO'x, Trabalhadores por Conta de Outrem) for that year.

---

(1) MESS, O Peso das Profissões Informáticas no Emprego e suas Perspectivas Futuras, Departamento de Estatística do Ministério do Emprego e da Segurança Social (Chapters II, III, IV).

2. Labour market

2.1. Actual employment of IT professionals

As can be seen from the following table, operators (O) are the most largest category, followed by Programmers (P) and Data-Entry Operators (OR) and, lastly, Analysts (A).

In general, the majority of IT professionals are included in this category, as it is the most comprehensive from the standpoint of the present function of small systems.

	A	P	O	OR	Total
Food industry	20	54	171	45	290
Textiles & clothing	48	97	129	34	308
Printing & publ.	42	30	128	73	273
Chemistry	54	105	206	94	459
Iron & steel	38	47	47	31	163
Metal industry	93	123	271	179	666
Energy	33	55	49	88	225
Construction	16	22	132	24	194
Wholesale trade	199	329	638	274	1 440
Retail trade	23	76	250	44	393
Transport	38	37	209	63	347
Communications	2	11	114	330	457
Banking & finance	237	242	2 101	1	2 581
Insurance	86	73	191	0	350
Company services	108	156	332	125	721
Others	70	116	305	152	643
TOTAL	1 069	1 526	5 226	1 526	9 347

The sector in which the largest number of IT professionals are employed is "Banks and Other Financial Institutions" with 2 581 staff (27.6 % of the total). There are also a considerable number of Operators (2 101) but no Data-Entry Operators in this sector.

The two next most representative activities are "Wholesale Trade" and "Real Estate Operations and Other Services".

In 4th place comes the "Manufacturing of Metallic Products and Machines" with 7.1 % of informatics employees. The majority of the enterprises in this sector (78) employ more than 100 workers.

2.2. Development prospects

It is difficult to predict the development of informatics at present owing to the current technological innovations in hardware and software developments.

However it seems possible that:

- the relative numerical importance of IT professionals, especially Programmers, will decline and the profession of Data-Entry Operators will disappear.

- a higher level of technical know-how and specialization will be required of IT professionals, and this may lead to a greater diversification of functional content and, consequently, of the designation of professions.

As to Portugal, the figures presented refer to two consecutive years and do not, therefore, constitute a series that can serve as a reliable guide to the future of the professions under consideration.

On the other hand, and as far as we know, no study has been conducted on the recent tendencies affecting installed hardware and the relationship between acquired hardware and the applications/activities for which it was intended.

Nevertheless, an analysis of the values obtained reveals two significant aspects:

- a decrease in the number of workers in every category with the exception of operators;

- a decrease in the average number of IT professionals per enterprise owing to their very slow increase compared with the number of enterprises that have created jobs in informatics.

2.3. Labour supply and demand

Although IT is recognized as an important factor for national development, qualified technicians are needed to exploit it and these do not exist in sufficient numbers.

Analysis of the situation based on the available information and a consideration of demand reveals that:

- The CTT Telecommunications (PTT) has approved an investment plan worth 150 million contos for a period of 4-5 years. In this context, 900 engineers will eventually be engaged over the next 3 years.

- The EDP (Portuguese Electricity Company) expects to take on 60 engineers per year.

- Siemens is organizing a Software Centre, for 200 engineers will be required.

- Standard Electric will also need 100 engineers for a software centre.

- Philips has a centre for 60 engineers.

These enterprises alone will recruit some 1 400 engineers over 3 years.

As regards requirements in other sectors - Banking, Insurance, Public Administration, Social Security, Armed Forces, Hospitals, etc. - and the National Institute of Statistics (which will require many IT professionals to staff the Data Collection Network it is to set up) - the demand will rise far beyond the capacity of the Portuguese Universities to produce graduate engineers.

The demand for graduate engineers accounted for 23.5 % of the vacancies advertised in the weekly "EXPRESSO" in the last quarter of 1987.

Over a given period, about 1/4 of engineering vacancies are in electrotechnology and electronics (the percentage varying between the extremes of 11.8 % in the 2nd week of January and 36.4 % in the 1st week of February 1988).

A knowledge of informatics, stressed in 17 % to 28 % of all job advertisements, is of definite advantage to candidates.

Sketching an identikit picture of requirements, based on data from the last quarter of 1987, an "EXPRESSO" analysis reveals the following candidate profile: between 30-35 years of age, previous professional experience, knowledge of English and of informatics as a user.

The demand for IT experts (analysts, programmers, etc.) accounts for some 6 % of all the advertisements published in that weekly.

3. Some characteristics of IT professions

3.1. Salaries and working hours (2)

To begin with, it should be pointed out that the overall relationship of the average basic salaries of informatics workers to those of all other employees in the QP was 1.52 in 1985 and 1.56 in 1986.

In 1985, the salary range of IT staff per activity, went from a minimum of $28 795 (Average Basic Salary in Agriculture and Hunting) to a maximum of $60 475 in Insurance.

In 1986, the values were $33 333 for the former and $74 010 for the latter; the 2.1 pay differential in 1985 increased to 2.2 in 86.

An analysis based on groups of professions and company size reveals that:

- Analysts and Programmers enjoy an average basic remuneration and earn above the average for IT professionals, by contrast with Operators and Data-Entry Operators. This finding is valid irrespective of company size.

- In both cases, remuneration generally decreases the smaller company concerned.

- Between 1985 and 1986 the Average Basic Salary increased by 22 %. In both cases, in enterprises with more than 50 employees and for all groups of professions, the salary increases were equal to or above the average, with the exception of Data-Entry Operators and Programmers - where increases equal to or above the average occurred in enterprises employing fewer than 50 staff.

---

(2) API, Informática Hoje, Associação Portuguesa de Informática (Chapter IV), April 1988.

- As to the relationship of earnings to average basic remuneration, which reflects the importance of additional remuneration (subsidies, overtime payments and other remuneration), this was 1.6 in 1985 and 1.8 in 1986, thus representing in both years, a value above the average in enterprises with more than 100 workers.

- In the case of the professions that relationship rises above average only for Operators; this is probably due to shift subsidies, night work or work done on free days which is a requirement of large enterprises, in particular, where computer work is practically nonstop.

Lastly, the academic qualifications of IT professionals must be considered.

A comparative analysis of their average monthly remuneration (earnings) with that of all other employees in the Continental QP shows that this is superior in the case of professionals with academic qualifications at least of High-School leaving standards, the reverse being true in the case of professionals with the baccalaureate or university degrees.

Within the IT professions themselves it can be seen that, in general, remuneration increases in line with higher academic qualifications.

Diffferences in remuneration between men and women were revealed with a clear advantage for men in almost every profession with the exception of Data-Entry Operators where women earn more.

Another distinguishing feature of IT professions is the number of working hours per week.

The average working week of IT staff was 37.2 hours in 1985 and 36.2 hours in 1986, representing an average decrease of 1 hour (approximately 2.7 %). Since there was a proportional change in the national average over the same period (1985-1986), the improvement in this professional sector can be considered to reflect national developments.

It should also be noted that, in 1985, IT professionals worked an average of 2.8 hours per week less than all the other workers covered by the QP and that this difference was mantained in 1986.

Whereas total overtime averaged 5 hours/week both in 1985 and 1986, the figure for IT professionals was of 3.7 hours/week in 1985 and 3.9 in 1986.

4. Government policy

4.1. National legislation on privacy and data protection

Article 35 of the Portuguese Constitution introduces a number of concepts giving rise to a need for regulation by the ordinary law which are, as a result, practically worthless, and merely provide a basis for future legislation.

The article in question refers to the right of access to the information stored in data banks and a right to notification of the purposes for which it is used. It prohibits access to personal data files and exclusively personal data held outside the country. It also forbids the processing of data relating to philosophical and political conventions, party or union affiliation, religious creed or private life in general. However, it is for the ordinary law to define the concept of personal data for purposes of IT storage and the fact that this has not yet occurred prevents an effective application of the article.

4.2. Legal protection concerning software copies

The first problem to be faced by a great number of enterprises which market legally acquired software concerns copyright protection or software licensing. In Portugal, neither the ownership nor the authorship of computer programs is regulated and they do not figure in the Copyright Code published in August 1985.

Portuguese software importers (who also market the product), pay copyright fees in the exporting country (as a result of the legal protection which those programs enjoy). This protection does not extend to Portugal. Our legislation neither provides for nor permits such an extension. The Copyright Code establishes that it is the exclusive responsibility of the Portuguese legal system to protect the works of foreign authors or works originating in a foreign country.

Another problem arises from the absence of specific legislation governing IT professions and access to them, which precludes control - all the more so as neither our Commercial Code nor the ensuing legislation take account of these activities which are in a constant state of development, require careful consideration and give rise to extremely competitive enterpreneurial attitudes to the conquest of markets.

UNITED KINGDOM

Tim BRADY
Science Policy Research Unit (SPRU)
Sussex University, Brighton

1. Definition of "information technology" (IT) professionals

It is extremely difficult to provide a strict definition of the term "IT professional". There is a lack of official statistics and companies do not necessarily collect and keep occupational data and may, in any case, have entirely different names for jobs involving similar tasks. The definition used by the Institute of Manpower Studies (IMS) in their research on IT manpower provides a useful guide (1). IMS developed an "occupational framework" consisting of two dimensions: activity or function, and skill/knowledge base. Within this framework, eight main functional areas were developed as follows:

- research, design and development;
- production;
- test and quality assurance;
- communication & distribution;
- marketing, sales and customer service;
- finance & accounting;
- other data processing;
- other (as specified).

---

(1) Connor H., Pearson R., <u>Information Technology Manpower into the 1990's</u>, Institute of Manpower Studies, April 1986.

There were also eight occupational groupings:

- software & systems engineering;
- communications engineering;
- electronics and product engineering;
- research and design specialists;
- marketing & technical sales;
- customer service;
- computing;
- other professionals, technicians with IT skills.

2. The Labour Market

2.1. Output of the education system

In the UK Universities and Polytechnics, there are no information technology first degrees as such, but there are a number of first degrees which can be called "**IT subjects**" in that they contain elements relevant to IT. In particular Computer Science, Mathematics, Physics and Electrical & Electronic Engineering can be considered IT subjects. In addition there are a number of IT courses at postgraduate level including **conversion courses** from non-IT disciplines (e.g. science, arts or social science). The IT conversion courses were the result of a major government initiative in 1982. In 1982/83 fewer than 200 students received awards from the SERC (the Science and Engineering Research Council), which is responsible for managing the initiative. However, the figure increased to about 800 students in 1983/84 and slightly more in subsequent years. The total number of IT conversion students is boosted by some employer-sponsored students and others who obtain Manpower Services Commission (MSC) funds.

In addition to the conversion courses, there are a number of advanced postgraduate **IT courses** approved by the SERC and aimed at people with first degrees in IT-related subjects. In 1983/84, there were 30 such courses, all but one at universities. In broad categories, 6 of these 30 were computing courses, 13 were microelectronics courses and the remaining 11 covered other subjects (2).

---

(2) Connor H., Pearson R., <u>Labour Market for IT Postgraduates</u>, IMS Report n[118, 1986, p 10.

Outside of higher education, training and education in computing skills takes place below degree level via a wide range of college- and industry-based courses which may be full-time or part-time, short-term or medium-term. Some of these courses, such as those run by the City and Guilds London Institute (CGLI) or Business and Technician Education Council (BTEC), lead to the award of formal qualifications Computer Studies has become a very popular subject at '0' and 'A' level during the 1980's (3).

2.2. Employment and unemployment of IT professionals

There are no comprehensive statistics on the employment of IT professionals in the UK. As far as official statistics are concerned, the 1981 Census of Population indicates a total of 129 000 people (of which 18 000 were women) people who could loosely be categorized as IT professionals, although this probably underestimates the true total. The 1984 New Earnings Survey does not distinguish between electrical and electronic engineers and estimates that there were 108 000 in this category in April 1984. The same survey estimated that there were 93 000 full-time male computer programmers and systems analysts (the sample was too small to allow estimates of women in these occupations). Thus, all one can really say from the official statistics is that the number of IT professionals is far in excess of 60 000 and probably nearer 200 000.

Luckily, there have been a number of surveys in the UK which have attempted to make reliable estimates of the total number of IT professionals. A NEDO report published in 1980 included estimates of manpower (4).

It was thought there were 60 - 62 000 professional electrical engineers (including managers) in electronic systems-related work and a further 90 000 employed in computing-related occupations, such as programmers and analysts. The 1985 IMS survey (5) estimated a total of around 200 000 IT professionals, of whom approximately 70 000 were in electronics-related occupations and about 130 000 in computing occupations. Subsequently, IMS have revised their estimated based with reference to a new survey of 143 organizations and a growth rate of between 5 and 10 per cent per annum, so that in 1987 they put the total number of IT professionals at 230 000 (6).

---

(3) Mason G., <u>Trends in Computing Qualifications in Secondary, Further and Higher Education</u>, Engineering Industry Training Board, May 1987.

(4) Anderson and Hersleb, <u>Computer Manpower in the 1980s</u>, NEDO 1980.

(5) Connor H., Pearson R., <u>Information Technology Manpower into the 1990s</u>, IMS, 1986.

(6) Pearson R., Connor H., Pole C., <u>The IT Manpower Monitor 1988</u>, IMS, 1988.

The National Computing Center (NCC) surveyed some 640 computer user organizations employing around 11 000 IT staff (including data-preparation staff and operators). The NCC extrapolated from these findings to produce estimates of the current size of the UK "**IT population**": 266 500 (7). This is forecast to rise to 293 900 in 1989 and 303 300 by 1992. These estimates relate to computing staff rather than to IT professionals and therefore do not cover all the electronics engineers included in the other estimates. Nevertheless, the Policy Studies Institute has recently estimated the number of engineers with microelectronics experience in the UK at 81 000 (8).

2.3. Case Studies with regard to IT professions

The pattern of IT employment varies within different end sectors. The Institute of Manpower Studies distinguished between four main **user groups** in its 1986 study of IT manpower: providers of electronics products and systems; providers of IT services; industrial users of IT; service users of IT.

Nearly a third of the electronics supplies companies employed more than 100 IT professionals. The IMS report notes that concentrations of over 1 000 IT professionals in a single location "were not exceptional in some of the major electronics companies" (9). In the IT service-providers sector, one in eight firms employed more than 100 IT professionals. The concentration of IT professionals was much smaller in the user firms: 74 % of industrial user organizations and 48 % of service users employed 20 or fewer IT professionals (53 % of industrial users employed fewer than 6 IT professionals). Some 15 % of industrial users and 16 % of service users employed more than 100 IT professionals.

In terms of size, the larger organizations in all sectors tended to employ higher numbers of IT staff: more than half the organizations with a total workforce of more than 1 000 employed more than 50 IT professionals. About one-third of medium-sized (101 - 1 000 employees) organizations employed more than 50 IT professionals, as did one in eight small organizations.

---

(7) Buckroyd B., Cornford D., <u>The IT Skills Crisis: The Way Ahead</u>, NCC, 1988.

(8) Northcott J., Walling A., <u>The Impact of Microelectronics: Diffusion, Benefits and Problems in British Industry</u>, Policy Studies Institute, 1988, p 80.

(9) Connor H., Pearson R., op. cit. p. 23.

There were differences in the **pattern of occupation** across sectors. In the case of electronics providers and industrial users, occupations were more orientated towards the following electronics and engineering occupational groupings: software & systems engineering; communications engineering; electronic and product engineering; research & design specialists; marketing & technical sales; computing; other. In the IT service-providers and service-users sectors, the occupational groupings were more orientated towards software skills: programmers; analyst/programmers; software & systems engineers; electronics engineers.

Computing occupations dominate IT professional employment among IT service-providers (94 %) and service users (82 %). Industrial users also have a high proportion of their IT staff (46 %) in computing occupations. As might be expected, the proportion of electronics engineers is small in the IT service-providers and service-users sectors (2 % in both cases). Not surprisingly, electronics providers were the major employers of electronics engineers and software/systems engineers (25 % and 28 % of employment), followed by industrial users (11 % and 20 %); 20 % of IT professionals in the service-users group were software/systems engineers.

2.4. Labour market regulation processes

The general shortages of IT professionals have, to some extent, created a suppliers' market. Recruiting and retaining highly skilled staff has been a problem in many sectors. This has led to a situation where the poaching of trained staff has become prevalent. Employers have come up with a number of responses to attract and retain their IT staff, including changes in grading structures and salary progression systems and alterations in the review procedures.

3. Social aspects and trends

3.1. Skills and tasks and work organization

The **skills** needed by IT professionals vary depending on the job they are doing and where they are working. The 1985 IMS study pointed to the wide range of skills needed to develop and apply IT, depending on the sector in which professionals worked. In their survey, they found that the abilities most needed by electronics providers were design and development skills for microelectronics, software or systems. In the IT service-providers group, the emphasis was on software skills. In the user sectors, DP and computing skills are those most in demand. Recently, there has been a decline in in-house programming in certain organizations as they have begun to purchase software packages. This has led to a shift towards systems-analysis skills.

In its 1987 survey (10), the NCC referred to a number of distinct technological trends which were likely to have implications for the skills of DP/IT staff. In particular, it mentioned the growing use of fourth-generation computer languages and relational data-base techniques. These were thought to be the major driving force behind a **deskilling of pure programming work**: fourth-generation languages automatically generate code which can speed up the process considerably and may not require high-level programming skills. The NCC also noted the growing need for analysis skills. It points to the rise of the **programmer/analyst** - a sort of systems-development all-rounder who has both business and analytical skills plus some programming expertise. In many cases, the IT department is being reorganized around this analyst/programmer role and the trend is for more analyst/programmers to be employed in the future at the expense of pure programmers.

The NCC report commented on a shift of emphasis in **systems development** resulting from the transition from solely "traditional" bulk data processing (i.e. the computerization of large-scale clerical tasks) to IT applications (i.e. a diverse range of applications at several levels: corporate, departmental and personal). These newer applications tend to have more complex effects on the organization: they are used to assist decision-making and to improve communications with the aim of increasing competitiveness; end-users are likely to be managers rather than clerical staff. The systems are more closely related to business activities and strategic factors and, hence, the people involved in the design and implementation of such systems need to be more "au fait" with the environment in which the business is operating. In short, there is a need for business skills in addition to (and in some cases rather than) technical skills.

---

(10) Buckroyd B., Cornford D., The IT Skills Crisis: the Way Ahead, NCC, 1988.

A fourth area of growing need was for **communications and networking skills**. People with such skills were regarded as specialists in much the same way as systems programmers have been regarded as specialists in the past. The important expertise is the technical knowledge required to design and implement communication networks.

The growth of end-user microcomputing has led to a requirement for a new type of **end-user support** from the DP department in many organizations. This support can take the form of help in choosing hardware or software and training end-users. The skills needed for this support role may differ considerably from those normally associated with systems development in the DP department. Specifically, technical knowledge of micro-operating systems, communications and microcomputer software packages, together with the non-technical skills of smooth communication with end-users, training ability and a knowledge of the business activities of the end-user department are required.

The NCC report (11) also pointed out the special skills requirements applicable to small installations where one person may well have to combine roles which are separated in larger organizations. Thus, one person could be responsible for analysis, programming, and support.

The Policy Studies Institute has undertaken a series of surveys on the use of microelectronics in UK manufacturing industry. The latest of these (12), covering some 1 400 factories, makes a number of comments on skills. The most acute need was for engineers with microelectronics experience. Half the factories in the sample using microelectronics cited a lack of people with microelectronics expertise as a very important problem, indeed it was mentioned spontaneously by more of them than all the other factors combined. It was perceived as the major difficulty in the introduction and use of microelectronics technology by all plants, irrespective of size, region, industry, or ownership, by those using the technology on a large scale, a little or not at all: by plants with product applications and by those with process applications.

---

(11) Buckroyd B., Conford D., The IT Skills Crisis: The Way Ahead, NCC, 1988.

(12) Norhtcott J., Walling A., The impact of microelectronics: Diffusion, Benefits and Problems in British Industry, Policy Studies Institute, 1988.

3.2. Types of work contracts and careers; professional mobility

As might be expected in a field where skill shortages are commonplace, there is evidence of high mobility. The NCC report on the IT Skills Crisis noted a very high turnover rate for the DP professions, especially for systems analysts, analyst/programmers, programmers and systems programmers. Turnover rates are higher in London and the South-East than in other regions of the UK. In terms of industrial sector, engineering and manufacturing had a high turnover with particularly high loss rates. Other sectors had lower loss rates but boardly similar recruitment rates. The Finance and Business Services Sector showed a relatively low loss rate but a high recruitment rate as did Distribution (13). The smaller the installation, the higher the loss and the lower the recruitment rate.

In their 1985 survey, the Institute of Manpower Studies covered a wider range of IT professionals than DP specialists alone. They found that the overall level of wastage was generally low - half the companies reported wastage levels below 5 % for all IT professionals. However, one in seven reported wastage levels of 15 % or more. Wastage rates tended to be higher in IT service organizations, with fifty reporting rates of over 15 %. The larger organizations had higher wastage levels than the small ones - 70 % of organizations with more than 1 000 employees had wastage levels for professional IT staff in excess of 5 % and fifty of them had wastage levels in excess of 15 %. When broken down by occupational level, programming/systems analyst occupations had the highest wastage rates and engineering-related occupations the lowest.

3.3. Training and Retraining Requirements

A survey of training carried out in 1984 by Occupational Services Ltd (14) found that 51 % of the respondents has a formal training policy, 67 % had a formal training budget, 41 % had a full time training officer and 39 % had a training department. Many employers of computer personnel carried out little or no formal initial training (fewer than 50 % had a set training-course for trainee programmers, only 15 % and 13 % had a set training-course for trainee analyst programmers and trainee systems analysts respectively). The larger the number of computer personnel employed by an organization, the more likely it was that set training programmes would be provided for trainees.

---

(13) Buckroyd B., Cornford D., The IT Skills Crisis: The Way ahead, table 3.1.3.

(14) Spurgeon P., Patrick J., Michael I., Training and Selection of Computer Personnel, Occupational Services Ltd., April 1984.

Continuing training for experienced employees, in the form of refresher or conversion courses was provided by 39 % of employers for programmers, by 44 % for analyst/programmers, and by 30 % for systems analysts.

Various training sources were used. For each of the three job categories at both trainee and experienced level, the source most used was other computer firms' courses, followed by in-house training facilities. Few organizations used educational courses. The report noted that an increasing amount of training, whether provided in-house or supplied externally by other organizations, was being carried out on the basis of self-instruction using manuals, visual aids and computer-assisted learning methods.

The NCC survey revealed that a third of the organizations in the sample had not recruited any trainees at all in the previous two years, reinforcing the impression that poaching is the preferred method of recruitment in a large number of organizations.

The CEL report for ITSA (15) found that the majority of trainee recruitment was undertaken by larger organizations - i.e. those with more than 40 DP staff - and that it was highest in the very large installations. The source of trainees was found to vary by industry group. The preferred source of recruitment for trainees across all industries was graduates, followed by people who had been on training courses, and then internal transfers. However, in the High-Tech sector (including DP equipment manufacture, electronic and instrument engineering, communications) and the Computer Services sector (comprising computer bureaus, software houses and other non-financial services) a very high proportion of firms taking on trainees make graduates their first choice.

The 1985 IMS study found that the majority of organizations tried to recruit a mix of new graduates and experienced/skilled IT staff to meet their needs. There were organizations which relied solely on recruiting experienced personnel. Apart from graduates, it did not identify the source of trainees. It did, however, discover the main sources used for new recruits' initial training and for the continuing training of experienced IT professionals. More than 70 % of IT provider organizations (both hardware and software) used in-house training facilities compared with less than half of the user organizations. User organizations relied more on manufacturers/suppliers' courses. Overall, only 21 % of organizations used facilities in higher education as a main source of initial training.

---

(15) CEL, Changes in the employment of IT staff, Computer Electronics Limited, August 1987.

A minority of the electronics providers still adhered to a formal graduate-trainee scheme, lasting up to two years, which could include periods of in-house training either within the training school or as on-the-job training in different parts of the company, and some external courses at manufacturers' premises. In the majority of companies there is little formal training, and this mainly takes the form of informal on-the-job instruction.

Many of the IT service-providers used their training facilities, which had been developed primarily for customer training, for their new graduates and other staff. There were a few examples of graduate training lasting up to a year but, on the whole, instruction was restricted to short periods of induction training followed by informal on-the-job training in the course of project activities.

There were few IT user companies providing extensive initial training. The main exceptions were organizations in the service-user sector, such as the Civil Service and some financial institutions where there has long been a tradition of resourcing computing-skill needs from within the ranks of existing employees or by recruiting school-leavers after "A" levels have been taken. The necessary IT training is provided in-house, together with occasional help from external sources such as training consultants. There were also a few exceptions in manufacturing, with some companies running extensive in-house formal training.

IMS found that, on the whole, continuing training for IT professionals was poor. What training existed was generally ad hoc and emphasized technical aspects. Little attention was given to long-term development.

According to a recent report from IT Strategy Services (16), in 1978, trainees accounted for nearly 50 % of all programming recruits and almost 25 % of all programmers in post. Since then, training and staff-development budgets have been redirected towards recruitment and salaries. In the private sector, only about 9 % of the IT workforce are trainees and the position is even worse - barely 7.5 % - in the public sector.

---

(16) Virgo P., Judd S., The State of the UK IT Skills and Training Market, IT Strategy Services, 1988.

3.4. Increasing professionalism

In September 1983, recognizing the need to give more attention to professional development in the computer industry, COSIT, the Computer Service Industry Training Council, launched a programme to stimulate recruitment and training and to raise professional standards in the industry. The 5-year scheme is called the Training and Career Development Programme and received backing from the Manpower Services Commission. The scheme, based on best practice in the computer services industry, is flexible and embraces both formal off-the-job and informal on-the-job training and related work experience. It is biased towards the first year of employment but is also designed to encourage subsequent training and career development.

There have been other moves than the COSIT scheme described above to improve the professional standards of IT professionals. In particular, the British Computer Society has been pressing for IT staff engaged in information systems engineering to become eligible for chartered engineer status. In order to facilitate this, the BCS has instigated the Professional Development Scheme (PDS), which is similar in concept to the COSIT scheme.

Another route to professional status now available is the Certificate in Software Engineering jointly introduced in 1987, by the Institution of Electrical Engineers and the National Computing Centre.

4. Government Policies

4.1. Education and Official Degrees

As part of a three-year programme announced in December 1982 aimed at strengthening the industrial and commercial use of IT in the UK and encouraging its acceptance and application, the government made provision for the expansion of education and training opportunities in IT. This included funding for additional places on first-degree, HND and HNC courses; grants for additional teaching and research posts in higher education; more postgraduate awards to support students in IT subjects - to be administered by the Science and Engineering Research Council (SERC); and extra funding for non-advanced further education to strengthen technician training. In terms of money, £ 38 million was earmarked for expenditure on these schemes between 1983 and 1986.

As a result of this initiative, the number of students on one-year postgraduate advanced courses in IT subjects rose from around 200 in 1982/83 to over 1 000 in 1983/84, and remained at this sort of level for the following two years. In 1985, the Government launched a £ 43 million Engineering & Technology Programme (called the "Switch"), designed to increase the number of places on first-degree and postgraduate course in a range of technological subjects, including computer science (17).

4.2. Role of Public Institutions or Agencies

The main government institution active in providing assistance or expertise on labour market issues has been the Manpower Services Commission. The MSC has provided funds for a number of computer-related training courses over the years. The MSC offered training to unemployed adults under the banner of the Training Opportunities Scheme (TOPS). Latterly, this has been replaced by the Job Training Scheme (JTS) and in recent years approximately 7 000 to 8 000 people have completed training courses in "technician/computer" skills under these schemes. The MSC was also responsible for assisting the funding of the Information Technology Centres (ITeCs) which came into being in 1981 and now operate in conjunction with the Youth Training Scheme. There are presently about 175 ITeCs training some 9 000 people in electronics, computing and electronic office skills. Since 1976, the MSC has funded unemployed school-leavers under the Threshold Scheme. This is run by the National Computing Centre, which claims to have trained some 11 000 youngsters in programming and the operation of commercial computer systems. Aimed at 17-19-year-olds, the scheme provides for the selection of trainees on the basis of aptitude testing and interviews, without regard to educational attainment. Surveys of Threshold trainees show that more than 80 % find jobs as computer operators or programmers (18).

We have already mentioned COSIT, the Computer Services Industry Training Council, and the grant-aided training scheme it offers to companies which are members of both COSIT and the Computer Services association. Once again, it is the MSC which provides the funding for the training grants. In addition to the Training and Career Development Programme, COSIT also administers other schemes eligible for grants.

---

(17) Mason G., op. cit. p. 27

(18) NCC, Output 1985/86, National Computing Center, p.2, cited in Mason G., op. cit.

Although finally established under the aegis of the Confederation of British Industry Education Foundation, the government was instrumental in Creating the Information Technology Skills Agency (ITSA) following the first report of the IT Skills Shortages Committee in 1984.

4.3. Government policy for IT professionals in public administration

There is little doubt that the skills-shortage problem has affected government both at national and local level. There are more than 300 government computer centres backed by over 15 500 staff. Within the Civil Service, there are no specific computer grades as such - posts in computing are classified as being appropriate to the level of responsibility and ability which is expected from a certain grade. Computer staff may be classified within the general administration group category and also under the open structure of the civil service [19]. The Government introduced Administrative Data Processing (ADP) allowances payable in addition to the normal salary for each grade, subject to a certificate of competency, in order to counter the problem of high salaries in the private sector and to encourage people to stay in the Civil Service.

At the local government level, recruitment and retention of IT professionals is still difficult. A recent report [20], based on research covering 16 local authorities, examined recruitment and retention problems and suggested possible solutions. Local authorities have introduced a number of incentives such as "golden hellos" (i.e one-off lump-sum payments) and market-related pay supplements on a six-monthly basis to attract and retain IT staff. Other incentives include mortgage-subsidy schemes, generous relocation packages, and leased cars. Other local authorities are trying to create more flexible grading systems for computer staff.

---

[19] The information on national government IT staff and pay in this section is taken from IDS Study 404, Computer Staff Pay, Income Data Services, February 1988.

[20] IDC, Salaries and Benefits in Local Government, Income Data Services and Peat Marwick Mc Lintock, 1988.

5. Professional associations and industrial relations

5.1. Role of Professional Groups and Associations

The main professional group is the British Computer Society. The scheme operated by the Computing Services Industry Training Council (COSIT) is in conjunction with one of the professional bodies, the Computer Services Association (CSA). The National Computing Centre Ltd. (NCC) claims to represent the interests of all sides of the IT community: users, manufacturers, service companies, government, and the many other professional bodies. It also claims to be the world's leading IT training organization with its courses and materials being used to train more students world-wide than any other independent company. It has been training professional IT staff, end-users, and managers since 1966. Some 18 000 students have been awarded the NCC Basic Certificate in Systems Analysis. Its training options include public courses, in-company courses, tutor-led training course materials packages, video awareness programmes, video self-instruction, computer-based training and interactive video (21).

5.2. Unionization of IT Professionals

There is no specific union for IT professionals. Where organizations are unionized, DP staff tend to join one of the white collar unions. The MSF (manufacturing, services and finance) union tries to recruit DP staff wherever it can in manufacturing and service industries. Firms in the computer services sector trend to be non-unionized, as do a number of (usually US-owned) hardware manufacturers in the UK. Other unions with computer staff in companies include APEX and BIFU, and ACTSS. In the public sector, computer staff are found in the Civil Service unions, NUCPS (National Union of Civil and Public Servants, CPSA (Civil and Public Servants Association) and IRSF (Inland Revenue Staff Federation) or in NALGO (Association of National and Local Government Officers).

---

(21) NCC, Training Courses 1988, NCC, 1988.

SELECTED BIBLIOGRAPHY

Belgium

Albertijn M., Baisier L., Wijgaerts D., *Informatie en overleg bij technologie-introducties*, Stichting Technologie Vlaanderen, SERV, Antwerpen, mei 1987.

Berleur J., Lobet-Maris C., Poswick R.F., Valenduc G., van Bastelaer Ph., *Les Informa-g-iciens: les professionnels de l'informatique dans leurs rapports avec les utilisateurs*, Presses Universitaires de Namur, 1986.

Coppe F., *Informatique: professions, formations*, SIEP, Bruxelles, pp 28-30

Crott R., Houard J., Claes P., De Bondt R., Sleuwaegen L., *Information, computer and telecommunication activities: statistical indicators for Belgium*, Services de Programmation de la Politique Scientifique, Bruxelles, 1987.

De Bondt R. et al., *Computer Industry in Belgium*, IBM-Belgium, 1986.

EURODATUM, *L'informatique dans les entreprises belges: les établissements informatisés et informatisables*, Etude réalisée pour et publiée par ASAB/VABI, Bruxelles, 1984.

Lobet-Maris C., *Informaticiens: de l'artisan à l'employé, les enjeux d'une mutation*, dans *Les Informag-i-ciens*, Presses Univ. Namur, 1986.

Lobet-Maris C., *Lien formation-emploi et stratégies des entreprises*, dans le Journal de Réflexion sur l'Informatique, n°7, octobre 1987, p 22.

SOBEMAP, *Ordiscopie* 1977, 1982, 1987.

Wilkin L., *Informatique et organisations*, Editions de l'Université de Bruxelles, 1986.

Denmark

Administrationsdepartementet, *Kontorteknik i staten - en laereproces*, 1986

Antonsen H., Strandgaard Pedersen J., *Computer Specialists - a survey*, CHIPS Working Paper 1988-10

Bansler, J., *Edb-faget industrialiseres - fanden tager de sidste*, in Lund-Larsen, Michael, *EDB-fagets fremtid*, PROBOG 1986

Björn-Andersen, N. & Malmvig, K., *EDb-specialister som professional gruppe*, IFA, Copenhagen Business School, 1977

Björn-Andersen, N. & Kumar, K., A Cross-Cultural Study of Information Systems Developer Values Relevant to Information Systems Development Submitted for publication in Communications of ACM

Borum, F. & Risberg, M., The IT-professionals: A statistical description, August 1988, Chips Working Paper n° 9

Christensen, P., Big brother i drifts-afdelingen, in Lund-Larsen, M., "EDB-fagets fremtid", PROBOG 1986

Danmarks Statistik: Statistiske Efterretninger, Uddannelse og kultur, 1987:5 & 1988:4; Statistiske Efterretninger, Arbejdsmarkedet 1988:12; Arbejdsmarkedsstatistik, 1987:4; Lön- og Indkomststatistik, 1982:1, 1987:1 and 1988:1

EDB-Rådet, Fem etiske regler for datamatikere, 1979

Folketinget, Lovforslag no. L 153: Forslag til lov om aendring af ophavsretsloven, 1987 & Lov om ophavsretten til litteraere og kunstneriske vaerker, Lovbekendt-görelse no. 52 af 27. januar 1987 & Betaenkning no. 1064, 1986"

Friedman, A., Strategies for computer people, September 1987, Chips Working Paper no. 3

Friedman, A., Understanding the employment position of computer programmers: a managerial strategies approach, October 1987, Chips Working Paper no. 8

Handelsskolerne, Edb-assistant uddannelsen, 1988/89

SAM-DATA/HK, Lönstatistik for edb-området, September 1987

SAM-DATA/HK, SAM-DATA's jobanalyse for juni 1988, 1988

Teknologisk Institut, Kvalitetscirkler på dansk, Tåstrup, 1988

Ireland

Brazil T.J., Wickhalm J., Engineering manpower in Irish Electronics: management perspective, NBST Report, 1987.

HEA, First destination of award recipients, Higher Education Authority, Dublin, 1986.

TCD, Electronic Surveys, Trinity College, Dublin, 1981, 1983 (University College Galway, 1985)

Wickham J., Trends in Employment and Skill in the Irish Electronic Industry, NBST Report, 1986.

France

Caillaux B., Peureux H., Les métiers de l'informatique, APEC, Collection "Demain les cadres", 1986.

CEREQ, Les professions de l'informatique, La Documentation Française, Paris, 1986.

Le Monde Informatique, Salaire de l'informatique, 13.04.87, Panorama des formations supérieures en informatique, 1.06.87, Le chômage en informatique, un léger mieux, 21.09.87, Un marché actif mais plus de chômage, 9.11.87, Marché de l'Emploi en informatique, une année faste, 25.01.88, Les mastères en informatique: une année utile, 22.02.88, Salaire de l'informatique, 25.04.88 et 27.06.88, Besoin croissant d'informaticiens mieux formés, 4.07.88.

Federal Republic of Germany

Bassler R., Informatiker im Beruf, in "Beitrage zur Arbeitsmarkt und Berufsforschung", vol 106, Nürnberg, 1987.

Dostal W., Mit Schirm, Chip und Konsole, Materialen zur Arbeitsmarkt- und Berufsforschung, Juni 1987, p 8.

Sandschepper G., Herr der Rechner: ein schwer regierbares Reich, in Online, n°6/1988, p 61

Streicher H., Karrierechancen für den DV-Profil, Online, n° 2/1988, p 80

Trautwein-Kalms G., Arbeitsbedingungen qualifizierter Angestellter, Arbeitspapier 22 der Projektgruppe, Humanisierung der Arbeit, Düsseldorf 1988, p 27.

Greece

Haikalis St., The Production of Microelectronics in Greece, Athens, 1982.

Jecchinis C., The Impact of Microelectronics on Employment, Athens, 1983.

Jecchinis C., What is the Impact of New Technology on Employment, Economicos Tachydromos, 8 January 1987.

Petriniotis X., The Employment of Women in Greece, in "Women's Employment and New Technologies", 1986.

Strategic International, Software in Greece, Confidential report, Athens, 1987.

Stratigaki M., Informatics and the Distribution of Employment by Sex, in "Womens' Employment and New Technologies", 1986.

The Impact of Employment from the Use of Electronic Computers, in Informatics in Greece, Athens, 1984.

Zafestos G. and Makris A., The impact of Electronic Computers on Employment in Informatics in Greece, Technical Chamber of Greece, Conference held from 3 to 6 April 1984.

Italy

Bellini R., Franchina G., Come cambiano le professioni informatiche, in "Management e informatica", Aprile 1987.

Butera F., Dalle occupazioni industriali alle nuove professioni, F. Angeli, Milano, 1987.

CENSIS (Centro Studi Investimenti Sociali), Informatica Italia 1986: mercato del lavoro, F. Angeli, Milano, 1987.

Della Rocca G., La formazione del rapporto di lavoro nelle attivita di produzione del software, mimeo, Milano, 1987.

ISFOL, Repertorio delle Professioni, Istituto Poligrafico dello Stato, Roma 1987.

The Netherlands

CBS, Automatiseringsstatistieken, Industriële Automatisering 1984-1986, Central Bureau of Statistics, The Hague, 1987. CBS, Overheidssector 1983-1984, The Hague, 1986. CBS, Particuliere Sector 1986, The Hague, 1988.

CHIP, Eindrapport (Final Report), Commissie Hoger Onderwijs Informaticaplan, The Hague, 1986

NGI, Functies in de Informatica, Rapport van de Werkgroep Functie-ordening van het Nederlands Genootschap voor Informatica (Functions in Informatics, Report of the Working Group Function-ordening of the Dutch Association for Informatics), third edition, Amsterdam 1988.

Roessnes D., Porter A., The Impact of Office Automation on Clerical Employment, 1985-2000, Georgia Tech Team, 1985

Trommel W.A., van Dam R., Vrouwen, industrie en automatisering (Women, Industry and Automation), Industriebond FNV (FNV reeks arbeid en technologie), Amsterdam, 1986.

Zanders H.L.G., Willems A.G., Office Automation in the Services Sector, CPI/KUB Tilburg, september 1987.

Portugal

API, Informatica Hoje, Associaçao Portuguesa de Informatica (Chapter IV), April 1988.

As maiores empresas de informatica, Cerebro, Ediçao Especial.

MESS, O Peso das Profissoes Informaticas no Emprego e Suas Perspectivas Futuras, Departamento de Estatistica do Ministério do Emprego e da Segurança Social (Chapters II, III, IV).

Spain

Castells M. & al., Nuevas tecnologias, economia y sociedad en Espana, Ed. Alianza, Madrid, 1986.

FUNDESCO, Formacion de tecnicos e investigadores en tecnologias de la informacion, Madrid, 1986.

Homs O., Kruse W., Ordovas R., Pries L., Cambios de cualificacion en las empresas espanolas, Fundacion IESA, Madrid, 1987.

Megia E., Vilarejo E., El papel de los interlocutores sociales en la formacion profesional en Espana, Study carried out for CEDEFOP (Berlin), Madrid, 1988

Segovia R., Zaccagnini J.L., Nuevas tecnologias y formacion ocupacional en Espana, FUNDESCO, Madrid, 1988

Villarejo E., Necesidades de formacion inducidas por las tecnologias de concepcion y diseno asistido por ordenador y software integrado de gestion, FUNDESCO, Madrid, 1988.

United Kingdom

Anderson and Hersleb, Computer Manpower in the 1980s, NEDO 1980.

Buckroyd B., Cornford D., The IT Skills Crisis: The Way Ahead, NCC, 1988.

CEL, Changes in the employment of IT staff, Computer Electronics Limited, August 1987.

Connor H., Pearson R., Information Technology Manpower into the 1990's, Institute of Manpower Studies, April 1986.

Connor H., Pearson R., Labour Market for IT Postgraduates, IMS Report n° 118, 1986.

IDC, Salaries and Benefits in Local Government, Income Data Services and Peat Marwick Mc Lintock, 1988.

Mason G., Trends in Computing Qualifications in Secondary, Further and Higher Education, Engineering Industry Training Board, May 1987.

Northcott J., Walling A., The impact of Microelectronics: Diffusion, Benefits and Problems in British Industry, Policy Studies Institute, 1988.

Pearson R., Connor H., Pole C., The IT Manpower Monitor 1988, IMS, 1988.

Spurgeon P., Patrick J., Michael I., Training and Selection of Computer Personnel, Occupational Services Ltd, April 1984.

Virgo P., Judd S., The State of the UK IT Skills and Training Market, IT Strategy Services, 1988.

publicity announcement

OFFICE FOR OFFICIAL PUBLICATIONS OF THE EUROPEAN COMMUNITIES

advertising space now available

under certain conditions (PTO)

publicity announcement

PUBLICITY QUESTIONNAIRE

The Commission of the European Communities has decided to open up a number of its publications to outside advertising. To find out more, or if you would like to place advertisements, please fill in this questionnaire and return it to:

OFFICE FOR OFFICIAL PUBLICATIONS OF THE EUROPEAN COMMUNITIES
2, rue Mercier, L-2985 Luxembourg

COMPANY: _____

NAME: _____

ADDRESS: _____

Tel.: _____

1. From among the publications listed below, please indicate the ones in which you would like to place advertisements:

☐ Euro-abstracts
Euratom and EEC R, D&D projects
monthly — A4 format
EN

☐ Supplement to the OJ
Public contracts
daily — A4 format
ES, DA, DE, GR, EN, FR, IT, NL, PT

☐ European Economy
quarterly —
A4 format
DE, EN, FR, IT

☐ Progress in coal, steel and
related social research
quarterly — A4 format
multilingual (DE/EN/FR)

☐ EC Bulletin
monthly —
B5 format
ES, DA, DE, GR, EN, FR, IT, NL, PT

☐ Energy in Europe
3 issues/year —
A4 format
ES, DE, EN, FR

☐ Catalogue of EC publications
quarterly and annual —
B5 format
ES, DA, DE, GR, EN, FR, IT, NL, PT

☐ Eurostatistics — Data
for short-term economic analysis
monthly — A4 format
multilingual (DE/EN/FR)

☐ Social Europe
3 issues/year —
A4 format
DE, EN, FR

2. Frequency of placement:

☐ in each issue of the chosen publication

☐ irregularly: number of placements _____

☐ (a) in alternate issues   ☐ (b) other (please specify): _____

3. Format of advertisement: ☐ 1 page   ☐ ½ page

4. Are you interested solely in advertising in the publications appearing in your native language or in all Community languages?

— Native language: _____
— Other languages: ☐ ES   ☐ DA   ☐ DE   ☐ GR   ☐ EN   ☐ FR   ☐ IT   ☐ NL   ☐ PT

Date: _____   Signature: _____

PLEASE NOTE:

The Publications Office reserves the right to reject advertisements it considers incompatible with the policy or aims of the Commission. The decision of the Publications Office is final.

Films (in very good condition) for offset printing must be supplied by the customer. The space taken up by the advertisement may not exceed the format indicated.

European Communities — Commission

Social Europe — Supplement
The labour market for information technology professionals in Europe

Luxembourg: Office for Official Publications of the European Communities

1990 — 162 pp. — 21.0 × 29.7 cm

DE, EN, FR

ISBN 92-826-1229-5

Catalogue number: CE-NC-90-001-EN-C

Price (excluding VAT) in Luxembourg: ECU 6.75